Love and Logic Magic® When Kids Leave You Speechless

Love and Logic Magic®
When Kids Leave You
Speechless

Love and Logic®
INSTITUTE, Inc.
800-338-4065 • www.loveandlogic.com

Jim Fay & Charles Fay, Ph.D.

The Love and Logic Institute, Inc.
2207 Jackson Street, Golden, CO 80401-2300
www.loveandlogic.com

First edition
First printing, 2000
Printed in the United States of America

Library of Congress Cataloging-in-Publication Data
Fay, Jim.
    Love and logic magic: when kids leave you speechless / from Jim and
Charles Fay—1st ed.
    p. cm.
ISBN 1-930429-04-5
1. Parent and child. 2. Parenting. 3. Manipulative behavior in children.
4. Communication in the family. I. Fay, Charles, 1964-II. Title.
    HQ755.85.F43 2000
    649'.1—dc21   00-010736

Publication Coordinator: Charles Fay, Ph.D.
Project Coordinator: Carol Thomas

Cover Design and Interior Design by Michael Snell,
Shade of the Cottonwood, Topeka, KS

Illustration by John Martin

TABLE OF CONTENTS

ALSO BY JIM FAY

Helicopters, Drill Sergeants and Consultants
Four Steps to Responsibility
Love Me Enough to Set Some Limits
I've Got What It Takes
Tickets to Success
Trouble-Free Teens
Pearls of Love and Logic for Parents and Teachers
Putting Parents at Ease

WITH CHARLES FAY, PH.D.

Love and Logic Magic for Early Childhood
Teacher in Charge
Calming the Chaos

BY CHARLES FAY, PH.D.

Oh Great! What Do I Do Now?

Order our complete catalog of stress-free
parenting and teaching titles:
1-800-338-4065
or visit our Web site:
www.loveandlogic.com

About the Authors

Jim Fay

J im Fay is one of America's most sought-
after presenters in the area of parenting and
school discipline. His background includes
31 years as a teacher and administrator, 20
as a professional consultant and public speaker,
and many years as the parent of three children.

Jim is internationally recognized as a speaker
and consultant to schools, parent organizations,
counselors, mental health organizations, and
the U.S. Military. He is the author of more than
100 articles, books, audios, and videotapes on
parenting and discipline. His infectious spirit and
sense of humor has made him a popular personality on radio and television talk shows.

About the Authors

Charles Fay, Ph.D.

D r. Charles Fay is a parent, Nationally Certified School Psychologist, and consultant to schools, parent groups, and mental health professionals across the United States. His expertise in developing and teaching practical discipline and behavior management strategies has been refined through work with severely disturbed children and adolescents in school, hospital, and community settings.

WELCOME TO OUR BOOK!

By Jim Fay

T his book is long overdue. For years participants in my audiences have asked that we provide a quick reference guide to dealing with the things kids say that leave us speechless.

I can't count the times when parents have said, "I just can't think fast enough to keep up with the things my kid hits me with!" Why does it seem so difficult to keep pace with our children these days? There are some very legitimate reasons why we have trouble responding to some of the perplexing, and downright frustrating, things kids say.

First, kids have the uncanny ability to recognize when parents are the most vulnerable, stressed, or guilt ridden. Have you ever noticed that your own kids rarely bring problems to you when you are the most prepared for them?

Second, youngsters have an amazing ability to read our body language. They take a look, do a quick analysis, and quickly realize which arguments will have the most emotional impact. With little effort, they soon learn exactly when and where to push our buttons, and they seldom waste their valuable time and energy arguing or manipulating around issues that their parents can handle easily.

Third, kids have more time to think about these things than we do! That's right. I don't have to tell you that parents lead a fast paced, time-consuming life full of responsibilities. These responsibilities leave little time and energy left over for considering how we might respond to exasperating things that come out of our children's mouths. For this very reason, we've made this book quick-to-read and practical.

Fourth, we often have difficulty knowing what to say because we worry that we might say the wrong thing—something that we might be sorry for later. No parent wants to say things, in the heat of emotion, which might just damage the relationship they have with their kids. This book gives some simple things to say—all designed to maintain such relationships.

Lastly, parents feel at a loss to say the right thing, or feel inadequate in the face of arguing, complaining, or manipulation, because kids typically play by a totally different set of rules during these times. The rules most parents play by go something like this: Be reasonable, loving, and fair. The children's rules read much differently: Win at all cost!

This book has been designed in a way that allows parents to get quick solutions to some of the most typical and concerning things kids say—and do.

CAUTION!

Before you experiment with the solutions we offer, please remember that the responses suggested are not designed to "get even" with kids or to "put kids in their place". If you use them for this purpose, they will make things worse. The message we constantly want to send our kids is this:

I love you too much to get angry, argue, or back-down.

The Love and Logic solutions included in this book are all designed to:
1. Keep the parent cool in the face of hot situations.
2. Show kids that arguing and manipulation are NOT effective ways of getting what they want or need.
3. Promote a home environment in which problems are discussed in respectful ways when both adult and child are calm—rather than when one or both are drunk with strong emotions.

We are offering many different examples. Don't allow yourself to fall into the trap of thinking that you need to memorize all of them. Pick a small number of Love and Logic responses, memorize them, and then hope for opportunities to practice them. The most effective parents we have ever met keep things very, very simple. They often rely on just one or two techniques and responses. Read this book, find your favorites, and enjoy!

This statement might raise the question, "Then why do you offer so many different examples in this book?" Quite simply, the more examples you experience, the more you will internalize the Love and Logic philosophy. As this happens, you will find yourself having a much easier time "living-out" this loving approach with your kids. Your Love and Logic responses will become automatic. You'll also get the wonderful bonus of having a lot less stress, and a lot more energy, at the end of each day.

A major energy and sanity saver is to realize that it takes two to tango. In other words, it takes both a child AND a parent to have a power struggle. Most children find it very boring and unproductive to argue with themselves. They need another player. Too often, adults get tricked into believing that they can come up with just the right words of wisdom to totally dazzle their kids. When was the last time you heard a kid say something like the following?

I was really mad and thought that all of this was just not fair. After you lectured me and got really stern, I now realize that life just isn't fair and that you are doing this for my own good. Boy, am I lucky to have such wise parents. And, I know this hurts you more than me. Give me a hug.

Let's make this simple and blunt. Arguing and lecturing with our kids DOES NOT WORK! What's the alternative?

MASTER THE ART OF GOING "BRAIN DEAD"

What? Brain dead? What does this mean? The more we think about what our kids are saying when they argue or manipulate, the more likely it will be that we will get sucked into the battle or possibly give in. As soon as you sense manipulation coming on, say to yourself, "Do not think. Do not think." Why? It's our own words that get us into the most trouble with kids. Our words become the fuel that runs a kid's arguing machine. Most youngsters have the ability to twist everything we say to their arguing benefit. Without our words, and bulging veins on our foreheads, arguing just fades away like dust in the wind.

Let's listen to a typical parent/child argument and see how the child uses the parent's own words as the fuel to power and continue the argument.

Parent: I told you that I'm not buying that toy for you.
Child: You don't love me.
Parent: Now you know that's not true.
Child: But you never buy me anything.
Parent: Oh, yes I do. Didn't I buy you a toy last time we went shopping?
Child: But you didn't get the one I really wanted.
Parent: I told you I couldn't afford that one.
Child: But you can always afford stuff for yourself.
Parent: That's out of line. I'm the one who earns the money.

Child: Well, how am I supposed to be able to make money?
           You make me spend all my time doing homework
           and chores. Besides, you should be paying me for
           my chores. You just make slaves out of your kids.
Parent: You know good and well that I don't treat you like
           a slave. You have very little to do around the house.
Child: Well none of my friends have to be slaves. Their
           parents love them and besides their parents aren't
           selfish! I didn't ask to be born into this stupid family!
Parent: That's enough of that, young man! I've had it with
           you. You're grounded! I don't know why you have
           to argue about everything!

As we analyze this argument, we find that both the child
and the adult are trying to out argue each other—they are both
dancing! The child is taking the lead by pulling the parent off
on a variety of "bird walks". What's the child's strategy?
Simply contradict each statement the parent comes up with.

Notice that, at no time, is this child about to say, "Oh,
wise parent, what you just said makes a lot of sense. I never
thought of it that way. I guess you're right after all."

Have you ever heard a child say these words? This is a
fantasy shared by many parents of the world, but it's only a
dream. Please give this fantasy a rest. It won't come true in
either your lifetime or mine.

There is a Love and Logic way to neutralize children's
arguing. Love and Logic parents simply go "brain dead" when
their kids start to argue. This typically involves calmly repeating
the same statement over and over. Soon the child realizes that
arguing doesn't get them what they want. Soon they realize
that arguing won't get them an entertaining display of parental
anger and frustration. Soon they realize that arguing is a waste
of time and energy.

Kids quickly abandon techniques that have a low rate of
return. For example, if a child's parents don't respond with
anger, concern, or "goodies" to temper tantrums, most kids
quickly give up on them. I know some parents who, upon

witnessing their toddler's first public tantrum, started clapping and encouraging. This display even encouraged a couple of other shoppers to start clapping. Their child's tantrum stopped rather quickly. And at last report, the parents say that they have not seen another. However, they tell me that the next time the youngster didn't get her way, she experimented with pouting. That didn't work for her either, so she moved on to dragging her feet and whimpering to herself. Since none of her experiments paid off, she has now moved on to being cooperative—because that works best of all for her.

Based upon these insights into the way children operate, let's replay the argument about buying a toy. This time the parent will use the "brain dead" approach.

Parent: I told you that I won't be buying that toy.
Child: You don't love me.
Parent: (In a very calm and sincere tone of voice) I love you too much to argue.
Child: But, if you loved me, you'd do it.
Parent: (Still calm and sincere) I love you too much to argue.
Child: Jessica's mom loves her. She buys stuff for her.
Parent: I love you too much to argue.
Child: You just learned to do that at that stupid Love and Logic course.
Parent: You're right. And—I love you too much to argue.

The Love and Logic responses included in this book are all designed to neutralize manipulation and arguing. They are NOT designed to be weapons in a battle to be won or lost by parents. This is not a game of "one-upmanship". Instead, these responses and solutions should be a very loving part of our goal to teach children a very important lesson. What is this lesson? Life's great rewards come through struggle and direct communication—not through manipulation.

WISE WORDS
Wise parents are consistently available to listen to their children when they hurt, are disappointed, or need advice. They teach their children how to approach them with sincere concerns, and they are always willing to discuss problems in a calm, loving manner.

As you learn to neutralize the manipulation and arguing with Love and Logic, use your new techniques with wisdom and sincerity.

......♥......

The Basics of Love and Logic

By Dr. Charles Fay

Building Life-Long, Respectful, and Joyful Relationships

I saw her in a local store. Her hair stood on end—as if she'd had her finger in a light socket for days. There were bags under her eyes and wrinkles the size of rivers in her forehead. At the end of her right hand was a small child. Suddenly, the silence of the toy aisle was pierced with a sound that sent shivers up and down my spine! Pointing persistently at the shelf of molded plastic, Junior wailed, "Mommy. I want that Alien Death Squad 2000 Mayhem and Destruction set!"

Exhausted, Mom frowned, looked down at her sweetness, and responded, "For crying out loud! I already said no. How many times do I have to tell you? That's got flying pieces. You'll lose them, and the dog will eat them, and—well—you'll put your eye out!"

Assuming verbal attack mode, Junior took a deep breath and blasted, "Why can't I? I want it. I want it! I want it. I want it! You never get me anything! I HATE YOU!" They argued back and forth for almost fifteen minutes!

Watching this scene, I was amazed at the creative arguments Junior devised! I was even more amazed, and dismayed, by how he used his words to change the color of Mommy's face.

A few days later a woman called me at my office. She was desperate for advice. She was desperate because she had just found drugs in her son's room, but he kept saying things like, "They aren't mine" and "Why don't you trust me?" and "This sucks!" Listening to her trembling voice, I once again realized the tremendous challenges parents face in today's world—and how many kids learn to wear their parents down through verbal brain drain.

Late that very same evening, little Marc, my son, sat across the table from me regurgitating peas onto his plate. Tears rolling down his face, he whined, "I hate this yuck."

THIS IS WHY WE DECIDED TO WRITE THIS BOOK!
NEVER BEFORE IN HISTORY HAVE KIDS
BEEN MORE SKILLED AT THE ART
OF VERBAL BRAIN DRAIN!

Our dream was to write a fun-to-read book full of practical parenting solutions. Solutions for kids of all ages, all designed to give parents strategies for avoiding arguments and power struggles! We asked each other, "Wouldn't it be great if a parent could pick up this book, read just a few pages, and get such useful ideas that they actually began to look forward to their kids starting to talk back or argue?"

We had another dream in writing this book—to help parents find ways to have as much fun as possible while raising happy, responsible kids. In other words, to help parents build life-long respectful and joyful relationships with their children. Many adults in today's society will do almost anything it takes to avoid visiting their parents. They say things like, "I can't stand them. They won't get out of my life!" or simply, "They drive me nuts!"

Wouldn't it be great if you and your kids, thirty years from now, still visited, laughed, and had fun together? Our philosophy of Love and Logic, the ideas we teach in this book, are all devoted to making this dream come true. From our experience with children and families, we've found that the first step toward making this dream a reality involves learning some practical skills for ending childhood arguing and manipulation—without using anger, lectures, or threats! One of these skills, of course, is the ability to listen and show you care when your kids are hurting and need compassion.

We decided to write a book full of simple, practical, time-tested solutions that parents can read quickly, use right away, and use with success. We decided NOT to write a book full of complicated theories or suggestions that were too general to really apply. That's why we've included twenty-three brief sections, each dealing with a different yet common parenting challenge. Some of these sections address relatively minor struggles, such as whining or temper tantrums. Others deal with more serious problems, like drug use. In each section, you will find specific examples and the actual WORDS to use when your kids leave you speechless.

This introductory chapter lays the foundation for everything else in this book. Finish this chapter first. Next, go to the table of contents, pick the section that covers the problem you are most concerned about, and cut right to the chase. For example, if your kids are fighting like cats and dogs, you may want to start with Chapter 19, entitled, "Brian won't stop picking on me! Make him stop!" Read this chapter, make a plan, and ask a friend to tell you what might go wrong with it. Why? Have you ever noticed how kids can find holes in our plans, slip through these holes, and leave us with egg on our faces? Friends, particularly other parents, can help us anticipate these problems, plug the holes, and give us the confidence to pull off our plan without breaking a sweat. The great thing about kids is that they're rarely boring! Sooner or later—probably sooner—they will come up with something new. Let's say that you get them to stop fighting, but one of them starts saying things like, "My friends don't have to do chores. Why are you so mean?" Go find this book, pull it back off the shelf, read Chapter 3, entitled, "None of my friends have to do chores."

How to get the most out of this book

STEP 1: Read this section first, so that you understand the basics of Love and Logic and how to go Brain Dead.

STEP 2: Go to the table of contents, and find the chapter that covers the current problem.

STEP 3: Read that chapter, and make a plan.

STEP 4: Tell your friends about this plan, ask them to help you anticipate what might go wrong, and plug these "holes".

STEP 5: Surprise your child with some new skills.

STEP 6: The next time your kids pull something, go back to the table of contents, find the chapter which best fits, and try something new!

WISE WORDS

*The best way of becoming a supreme master
at the art of neutralizing arguing is to read every section
in this book. Why? The repetition of seeing these
skills applied to twenty-three different problems
will help them become automatic for you.*

Before continuing, just what is this "Love and Logic" we
keep mentioning? Love and Logic is a philosophy and set of
techniques designed to put parents back in control of their
homes in a loving, kind way. Each idea and technique associated
with this philosophy is devoted to helping parents raise
responsible kids who are prepared to become happy, successful
adults. In the mid-1970s two men met in Evergreen, Colorado
and began to develop these ideas—Jim Fay, an elementary
school principal and my father, and Dr. Foster Cline, a child
psychiatrist. They noticed that raising kids was getting tougher
and tougher. In their quest to make it easier, they studied
research, analyzed really successful parents, experimented
with their own kids, and put their heads together—a new
and powerful way of raising children was born.

Love and Logic is based on four ideas or principles. Each
section in this book is designed to help you neutralize arguing,
AND each is based on these four basic principles.

The Four Basic Principles of Love and Logic
1. Help kids feel good about themselves.
2. Help them learn to solve problems and think for themselves.
3. Leave them with a healthy sense of control.
4. Teach them to be responsible for the consequences of
   their actions.

Helping kids feel good about themselves
Each and every idea or technique described in this book is
designed to help kids learn to feel good about themselves.
At the Love and Logic Institute, we believe that self-concept
building is an "inside job". In other words, we DO NOT

believe that the road to self-esteem is paved when parents do everything they can to make their children happy. And, we DO NOT believe that self-esteem is built when kids are given everything they want and are the recipients of constant praise. Instead, we know that children with the highest self-concepts have parents who:

1. Set limits in firm yet loving ways
2. Expect their children to do a fair number of chores around the house
3. Allow their kids to struggle with the consequences of poor choices—instead of rescuing them
4. Let their children see that they can solve their own problems and make wiser decisions as a result
5. Show them that manipulation and arguing are very ineffective ways of getting what they want out of life

Helping them learn to solve problems and think for themselves
For today's children and teens, the world is filled with more life and death decisions than ever. By the time many children are through the sixth grade they've already been confronted with tough decisions about drugs, alcohol, sex, and violence. Most people agree that kids need to be even better thinkers, at even younger ages, than ever before! How do we as parents make this happen? By giving them lots of opportunities to make reasonable choices, live with the consequences of these choices, and solve any problems created by these choices.

As you read each section in this book, you will notice that Love and Logic parents give lots of choices on matters that are not life and death. You will also notice that Love and Logic parents do discipline in a way that requires their kids to think more than them. How? When a child causes a problem, they ask with sincere empathy, "What are you going to do to solve this problem?" Love and Logic parents give caring guidance, but they don't steal learning opportunities from their kids by rescuing, threatening, or allowing themselves to get sucked into an argument. They know that the more a child argues, the less he or she has to think—and learn.

Leaving them with a healthy sense of control
Everyone needs to feel a healthy sense of control or freedom. In fact, control is a basic human emotional need. And when this need is not met, people will do almost anything to meet it—including argue and fight! Consider the American Revolution. Why was a small group of poorly armed citizens willing to risk their lives in battle? The answer? Control! Wasn't the Revolutionary War fought almost entirely because a group of people lacked a sense of control or freedom in their day-to-day lives? Sadly, revolutionary wars are being fought every day in homes across America. When kids lack a healthy sense of control, they will argue and fight to get it. What's the good news? Love and Logic teaches how to share control over lots of small issues so that we actually have MORE control over more important ones. This book is all about giving healthy bits of control rather unhealthy ones. When kids are able to manipulate their parents, argue, and be nasty, the control they receive is clearly not what's best for them—or anyone else!

Teaching them to be responsible for the consequences of their actions
At the heart of Love and Logic is a wonderful formula for teaching responsibility. It goes something like the following. First, allow your kids to make as many choices as possible on issues that won't cause a problem for anyone else. Secondly, hope and pray they make a few poor ones. Yes! Hope and pray they make mistakes! Why? Love and Logic teaches that the road to wisdom is paved with mistakes. What have you learned the most from? Your wise decisions or your poor ones? Most adults will admit learning a whole lot more from their poor choices than their good ones! Lastly, lock-in a strong dose of empathy or sadness BEFORE delivering any consequence. That is, show the child that you care for them first!

EMPATHY MUST ALWAYS COME BEFORE THE CONSEQUENCE!

Why is empathy so important? Let's take a look at two ways a parent might deal with an incident of accidental window breaking.

Example A

Dad: How many times do I have to tell you not to throw rocks around the house? This kind of thing really makes me mad!

Child: But Dad. I didn't mean to. It was an accident.

Dad: If you would just be a little more careful, these sort of things wouldn't happen. Just think about what you are doing!

Child: But I was!

Dad: You're paying for that window! I mean it!

Child: Not fair!

Dad: Listen, young man. Life isn't fair…(and so on)

Example B

Dad: (In a soft tone of voice) Wow. I bet you feel horrible about that window. How sad.

Child: But it was just an accident.

Dad: (Still in a soft tone) I know. How sad.

Child: Aren't you going to yell at me or something?

Dad: Why would I yell when you already feel so bad? I love you. What are you going to do?

Child: I don't know.

Dad: No problem. I bet you have just enough money to pay for it. Or, maybe you would rather do some extra chores and have me pay for it?

Child: I guess I'll just pay for it. But it's gonna cost a lot.

Dad: I know. Doesn't this stink.

Child: Yeah.

Dad: Give me a hug.

The following questions usually make it pretty clear which approach has the greatest chance of creating the most responsible, healthy kid:

1. Which kid would you rather be? The one is example A or the one in example B?
2. Which kid is NOT developing a long-standing resentment toward his father?
3. In which example is the kid thinking more about love than revenge?
4. Which kid will want to visit his parents when they are ninety?
5. Which kid is taking ownership of the problem rather than focusing on how mean he thinks his dad is?

If you answered example "B" to each of these questions you're right on track with Love and Logic! Among its many benefits, delivering empathy first allows parents to:

1. Hold kids firmly accountable for their actions without feeling guilty.
2. Maintain a loving relationship with their kids.
3. Model—and therefore teach—kindness and empathy.
4. Allow their children to think about the pain created by their poor decisions—rather than thinking about how "mean" or "unfair" the parent is.
5. Avoid a lot of verbal battles in the first place!

Over the past few years, our primary goal has been to make Love and Logic even simpler to understand and use. We know that parents have enough to think about without trying to remember the four basic principles or values. Further, we started to realize that almost all of what we teach can be summarized in terms of two simple rules:

The Rules of Love and Logic
1. Take care of yourself by setting limits without anger, lectures, threats, or repeated warnings. Show your kids that you can

handle them without getting angry.

2. Every time a child causes a problem, hand it back using a strong dose of empathy and then a logical consequence. The child should do more thinking about the problem than the adult.

Even more recently, we've realized that Love and Logic can be boiled down even further! About the time kids start to crawl, they begin experimenting to find out how the world works. This is normal and healthy! Some of their experiments are sweet, for example, "I wonder what will happen if I say please?" or "I wonder what will happen if I give Mommy a nice hug?" In contrast, some of their experiments are sour, like, "I wonder what will happen if I spit my peas across the table at Daddy?" or "I wonder what will happen if I lay on the floor here in the store and start screaming?"

Sadly, in some families, the parent's first reaction to these sour experiments is to warn, lecture, yell, or spank. In other words, the parent's first response is to show frustration and anger. Sadly, this entertaining show of parental exasperation sets in motion the following vicious cycle:

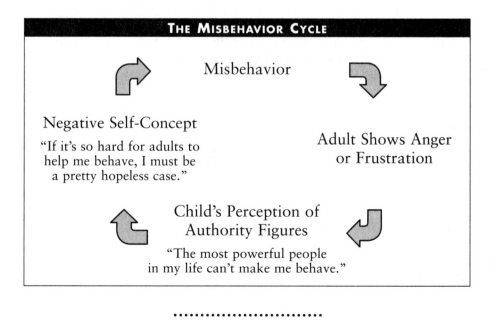

THE MISBEHAVIOR CYCLE

Misbehavior

Negative Self-Concept
"If it's so hard for adults to help me behave, I must be a pretty hopeless case."

Adult Shows Anger or Frustration

Child's Perception of Authority Figures
"The most powerful people in my life can't make me behave."

What message is sent to a child when their parents' initial response to misbehavior is typically frustration, anger, and lectures? Simply stated, the child begins to reason, "The most powerful people in my life—my parents—find it really difficult to make me behave. They must not be very strong." Even sadder, some children begin to believe, "Hey! It's entertaining to see my parents get frustrated. Let the fun begin!" The end result is typically a child who experiences problems with authority figures for the rest of his or her life. This is the child who enters the classroom and argues with the teacher. This is the child who grows up, enters the workplace, and finds it impossible to "tolerate" the boss saying things like, "Come to work on time" or "I need this job done by tomorrow." Why? Because the following belief was locked in this kid's noggin early in life: "Big people can't make me behave!"

Another sad result stems from parental frustration and anger. What happens when a child begins to realize that his or her parents can't handle him without frustration and anger? The child begins to view himself as bad and hopeless. Yes! The child begins to reason on a subconscious level, "If the most powerful people in my life can't make me behave without getting really mad, then I must be a pretty bad, hopeless case." When children begin to see themselves in this way, their behavior almost always matches this belief. The child begins to misbehave even more, and the cycle continues.

How's a parent prevent or break this cycle of low self-esteem and misbehavior? What does Love and Logic really boil down to?

SHOW YOUR KIDS THAT YOU CAN HANDLE THEM WITHOUT BREAKING A SWEAT!

That's right! Show your kids that you can handle them with both hands tied behind your back. When kids see their parents responding with empathy, instead of anger, lectures, threats, and warnings, they are forced to form this belief, "Wow! My mom can handle me without even getting frustrated! If she can do it this easy, then I must not be such a bad kid. There's hope for me!" This is Love and Logic in its simplest form.

How's a parent do this when their kids do or say something that leaves them speechless? Each chapter in this book is devoted to showing parents how to handle misbehavior without anger, without lectures and threats, without repeated warnings, and without spanking. What's the first step? If you don't remember anything else from this first section, remember this:

NEVER ALLOW YOUR KIDS TO PULL YOU INTO AN ARGUMENT OR POWER STRUGGLE!

Each chapter in this book outlines practical skills for neutralizing arguments and power struggles. Consider how much fun parenting can really be once you've become a black belt at the art of stopping back talk. Think of how much more energy you are going to have at the end of each day!

LOVE AND LOGIC

Easy to learn
Raises responsible kids
Changes lives
You can start right away

CHAPTER 1

WISE WORDS
*Wise parents never try to convince kids that their
decisions are fair.*

Let's start with a simple, quick example. "That's not fair!"
This is a favorite one for kids! Why do they use this one
so much? One reason is that it works so often. It doesn't
work all the time, but that's not the point. One characteristic
of humans is that we are easily captured by what psychologists
refer to as the variable schedule of reinforcement.

The masterminds at the gambling casinos know all about the variable schedule of reinforcement. They program their slot machines to let you win once in a while. Since you never know for sure when it is going to happen, you are enticed to continue putting in your money and pulling the handle. And you are always a little afraid to stop for fear that the next pull is going to win the jackpot. If the winning pull were to be predictable, the casino would be the loser and soon out of business.

The same thing happens with kids and the ways they try to control adults or get their own way. If pouting will get them what they want once in a while, it's worth trying it over and over, always with the expectation that the next pout will do the job.

As we mentioned, kids are actually amateur scientists. They constantly experiment with behaviors to "test the waters" with an eye for what works. They experiment with tantrums, pouting, complaining about fairness, refusing to talk, being overly sweet, begging, etc. until they find the one that works. Then they become like that gambler at the slot machine, pulling that handle over and over. They know that their technique won't work every time, but they also know that it might just work the next time. They realize down deep, "I can't give up now—because the next time might just do the trick!"

In future chapters, we'll discuss other reasons kids develop favorite manipulation maneuvers. And, you will have plenty of chances to increase your knowledge of child psychology. The more you understand, the easier it will be for you to consistently resist the urge to argue with your kids. The more you understand, the simpler it will be to help your kids learn that effort and honesty have greater payoffs than manipulation and arguing.

As we move toward this goal of helping children learn to be nice instead of nasty, the important concept is parental consistency. This does not require that you always say the right words, or that you are the "perfect" parent. Instead, it just means that you consistently show your kids that arguing doesn't get you mad AND doesn't get you to back down. You can do this in a number of different ways, using a variety of simple Love and Logic One Liners. Let's take a look at how a parent might use the One Liner "I know" to stop the "Not fair!" argument:

Child:	It's just not fair that I can't go to the party.
Adult:	(In a soft tone of voice) I know. (Brain Dead response followed by silence)
Child:	But all the other kids are going.
Adult:	(Still in a soft tone) I know.
Child:	I'm the only one who isn't going to be there.
Adult:	I know.
Child:	You are ruining my social life.
Adult:	(With gentle firmness) I know. You can tell them it's my fault if it will help.
Child:	Well it is your fault.
Adult:	I know.
Child:	Everyone will think I'm a dork.
Adult:	I know.
Child:	You don't love me. (Turning up the heat)
Adult:	(Silence)
Child:	You're mean, I hate you!
Adult:	I know.
Child:	That's all you can ever say!
Adult:	I know. I love you too much to argue.

FOR YOUR THOUGHTS

1. Who is forced to do most of the thinking in this interaction?
2. How long could the adult in this scenario continue to say, "I know"?
3. Does this approach guarantee that the child will not become frustrated? Or does it guarantee that the adult will not?
4. Is this child learning that manipulation doesn't work?
5. This parent stayed calm and used a soft, gentle tone of voice. Can you see how this approach would backfire if the

adult used the very same words but used them with an angry, frustrated, or sarcastic tone of voice?

CAUTION!

Most of the message we send is done NOT with our words but through our tone of voice and other nonverbal cues. When anger, frustration, or sarcasm creep into our words and actions, we run the risk of destroying the most important thing we have—our children's love and respect.

······❤······

CHAPTER 2

WISE WORDS
*Chores are the basic building blocks of pride
and feelings of being loved and needed by one's
family. Kids who have this at home don't need
to find it in a cult or street gang.*

One of the biggest mistakes parents make is paying their children to complete chores. Why is this such a mistake? First, paying them sends the following message: "Never do anything unless there is something in it for you." Secondly, pay for completing chores steals the sense of internal pride and accomplishment kids get from making meaningful contributions to the family. Instead of saying to themselves, "I did those chores because I'm important and needed," getting paid causes them to think, "I did those chores because I wanted five bucks."

WISE WORDS
Do not pay your kids for completing their chores.

Although chores help kids feel needed, important, and proud, almost all kids grumble about doing them—especially when there is no money involved. Some even resort to extreme measures such as "forgetting" to do them, doing a sloppy job, or even saying something irritating like, "None of my friends have to do chores." Why do we have so much trouble getting our kids to do jobs around the house? Many of us remember our own childhood, when forgetting to do a chore or resisting in any way was never even considered. Why is it that the vast majority of kids in the "good old days" did their chores without resisting, while the vast majority today would rather go for oral surgery than take out the trash?

It is clear to see that today's children are bombarded with a variety of messages from television, radio, and other media that in effect say, "It is really wrong and unfair to struggle, work, or wait for anything because you are such a special little human being." How often do we see kids in TV commercials have to work—or even wait thirty seconds—for the latest version of their favorite toy? That's not the way advertising works. Commercials only work if they convince kids that their parents should buy them whatever they want right away.

Besides messages beamed into our homes via TV and other media, kids also hear their fair share of propaganda from other kids in the neighborhood and at school. How often do we hear our kids saying things like, "Well, Joel's dad doesn't make him do all this work." The very sad reality is that such irritating comments might be true. How often do we hear of parents in our communities giving their children anything they want for little or no work in return?

WISE WORDS

When kids say, "Mary's mom doesn't make her do chores," wise parents smile and say, "Well that's really sad for Mary. Aren't you glad I love you enough to expect more of you?"

Lastly, kids are also more resistant to doing chores because households have become increasingly more hectic. Often with both of their parents working long hours, kids no longer spend much time watching their parents do chores around the house. Little kids used to watch their parents doing chores. Watching this, they thought to themselves, "That's what you do when you get big—I wish I were big like Daddy." Have you noticed how very young children always want to help? From this natural desire to help, little kids joined in and soon learned very early on that chores are part of life—and actually make you feel kind of proud and "big."

In today's world, most of us are so stressed by the end of the day that three things tend to happen. First, we just ignore our chores. Secondly, we do them but complain or communicate through our nonverbal expressions that we hate doing them. Thirdly, we pay somebody else to do them. In all of these ways, we model to very young children that chores are unpleasant and make big people feel bad. It's not surprising that our children's natural tendency to help soon subsides.

The good news is that busy parents can make an effort with their children to model having fun doing chores. When we understand how important chores are to lifelong success, it is easier for us to take the time to "whistle while we work" and have fun with our kids as they help us with some things around the house. Although difficult at the end of a tough day or week, this investment yields lasting gold for us and our children. Soon they begin to associate chores with love, fun, appreciation, and pride.

Wait a minute! What do you do if your kid is already older and you feel like it would take an Act of Congress to get him to take his plate to the sink?

WISE WORDS
Chores are so important to lifelong success that wise parents win the battle over them at all costs—for both themselves and their children.

A common parenting tip reads something like this, "Pick your battles wisely." In other words, don't fight battles with your kids over unimportant issues, and never start a battle you aren't willing to finish—and win! Wise parents realize that if they can't get their kids to do chores without reminders, their kids are learning more and more that adults are really powerless. Kids who learn this soon believe that their teachers can't make them do anything, the police can't tell them what to do, and the way you get what you want in life is by resisting people in authority.

WISE WORDS
Chores represent the basic foundation for cooperation with parents and other authority figures.

Let's look at an example in which a parent of an older kid took a stand on this issue and won—for both her and her child:

Parent:	Will you please mow the lawn?
Child:	I'm not doing it. None of my friends have to do chores.
Parent:	(In a sincere, calm tone) That's really sad for your friends. Aren't you glad that I love you enough to expect more of you?
Child:	Not really.

Parent: I still need you to do it.
Child: Well, this sucks.
Parent: (Softly) I know.
Child: Well, I'm still not doing it.
Parent: (In a sad tone of voice while walking away) I
           know. I love you too much to argue with you.

The parent drops the issue until she has talked with all of her friends and put together a plan that is so watertight that her boy will not be able to manipulate his way out of being responsible.

WISE WORDS
Wise parents delay consequences until they have time to talk to others and put together a "watertight" plan. These plans teach resistant kids that their parents are so powerful that they can handle them without breaking a sweat—and so loving that they can discipline with sadness instead of anger.

Monday morning.
Child: Mom! Somebody stole the bike you bought me!
Parent: (In a very soft, sad tone) Ohhhh. I had to pawn it.
Child: What! You can't do that! I'm calling the police! Why?
Parent: I didn't want to fight with you about the chores.
           So I pawned the bike to the neighbor—to get the
           money for paying someone to cut the yard.
Child: But that was my bike!
Parent: I know.
Child: But how am I gonna get to my friends?
Parent: I don't know.
Child: You better get it back for me!
Parent: (Still in a calm tone of voice) The good news is that
           you might be able to do enough extra work around
           the neighborhood, or take enough money out of
           savings, to buy it back.

Child: I hate you!
Parent: I know.

This parent did a number rather smart things to avoid an argument and deliver a strong yet loving dose of discipline. First, she held firm to her request, and she used some Love and Logic One Liners to avoid getting sucked into an argument. Secondly, she dropped the issue and took some time to get calm, talk to others, and put together a strong plan. Next, she delivered the consequence with sadness instead of anger. And finally, she resisted the urge to say something like, "Now have you learned your lesson young man?"

WISE WORDS

Every time we lecture a child about what he or she has learned, or say something like, "Now, have you learned your lesson?" we rub salt into the wounds and damage the parent-child relationship. Kids learn most from consequences when we keep our mouths shut and let the consequence be the "bad guy."

Let's take a look at another example in which the parent uses an even more sophisticated approach. Watch how this parent shares control through choices to avoid a power struggle:

Parent: You can either mow the lawn this week or clean the bathrooms. You decide which one.
Child: I'm not doing that stuff today.
Parent: Don't worry about it today. I just need one of those things done this week. Would you like to have it done by Friday or Saturday evening?
Child: I just don't want to do it.
Parent: I know. It's a bummer. I sure will appreciate it.
Child: Well, my friends don't have to do all these chores.
Parent: I know.
Child: But it's true!

Parent: (In a soft tone as the parent walks away) I know, and aren't you glad I love you enough to expect more out of you? Thanks so much! I appreciate the help!

Parent completely drops the issue until Sunday, prepared to pawn something or refuse to do something the child wants of her if the chore is not done.

Child: I did that dumb chore.
Parent: It is so nice to have your help! Thanks!
Child: I hated it! Why do I have to do those stupid jobs?
Parent: Why do you think?
Child: 'Cause you're mean?
Parent: (Smiling) If you don't figure it out by the time you have kids of your own, I'll sit down with you and explain it.
Child: You are so weird.
Parent: (With a big smile and a hug) I know!

FOR YOUR THOUGHTS

1. Is it possible that children either learn to like—or to hate—chores by noticing how their parents feel about them? Are you guessing that many kids learn to hate chores by seeing and hearing their parents complain about having to do them?
2. How long would you do chores for someone if they always criticized the way you did them? Is it important to focus on what our kids do right—and to let them know how much we appreciate their help?
3. Why is it a bad idea to pay your kids to do their chores?
4. Why is it important to say, "I'll be happy to listen when your voice is calm like mine"? Does this leave the door open for healthy discussion of the problem?
5. Why was the child in the second example above less resistant? Do you like it when your boss gives you some choices?

CHAPTER 3

WISE WORDS
Wise parents don't dignify the ridiculous by offering factual information.

Why are kids so quick to use the, "You don't love me" argument? The reason for this can be found in our deep-seated love for kids. Kids are born with an uncanny ability to sense what is most important to their parents. The great psychologist, Fritz Pearls, said it best when he wrote, "Four year old children are the best psychiatrists there are. At this age they have the ability to look at an adult, know immediately what is the most important value of that adult, and know exactly where and how to push the adult's button and watch him/her go crazy."

Dr. Pearls also taught us that humans lose about 70% of this ability by the time they become adults. I often wonder if endowing kids with this ability was our Creator's gift to children so that they could compete with the power of bigger people. At least we know one thing for sure, many children bring their parents to their knees. They do this by tricking the adults into an argument that can never be won by reason and facts.

A parent who engages in an argument about whether or not he/she loves the child is working under a severe handicap. First, the issue at hand is not really about love, but about the children trying to get the parent to give in. No amount of new information is going to make the child say, "Oh, I guess I was wrong about that."

The youngster in this argument is actually playing by a different set of rules than the parent. While the parent is trying to provide factual information and reminders of how his/her love has been shown in the past, the child is trying to get the parent to provide ammunition for escalating the argument. Any kid, worth his salt, knows that adults eventually run out of facts. And when they do, they get emotional. Once the adult gets frustrated and emotional, the adult loses. We will talk more about this in later chapters.

The following is an example of an adult trying to win an argument by providing factual information. Notice how the child uses each fact as a never-ending supply of ammunition.

Child: You don't love me.
Parent: Don't say that, you know it's not true. Aren't I
         always telling you how much I love you?
Child: But if you mean it, you'd buy me that doll.
Parent: But I'm always buying you things.
Child: But not the things I really want.

Parent:	Well, I don't have enough money to buy you every-thing you want.
Child:	But you always have enough to buy stuff for Jeffrey.
Parent:	Wait a minute! I spend the same amount on each of you.
Child:	Yeah, but last year you bought him a bike and that costs a lot more than this doll.
Parent:	OK. That does it! Now you're not getting anything the next time we go shopping. I've had it with you and your constant complaining!
Child:	See, I knew you didn't love me.

WISE WORDS

There's nothing wrong with a child that an arguing parent can't make worse.

Let's observe as a Love and Logic parent deals with the same issue.

Child:	You don't love me.
Adult:	(In a soft, sincere tone) How sad for you to think that.
Child:	If you loved me, you'd buy me that doll.
Adult:	(With a gentle smile) Nice try, pal.
Child:	But I really need that one.
Adult:	I know.
Child:	You're mean!
Adult:	I know.
Child:	You just don't love me.
Adult:	(In a calm, sad tone) How sad that you think that. It looks like it's time for you to spend some time in your room. Feel free to come out as soon as you can act nice. Thanks.

FOR YOUR THOUGHTS

1. How did the Love and Logic parent in scenario #2 avoid providing ammunition for the child's argument?
2. Who was in control of the discussion during the first scenario?
3. How might the child have reacted if the parent in the second scenario had responded with sarcasm?
4. Some parents have the ability to put their arm around their kid while saying, "Nice try, pal." Can you see this softening the interaction and establishing a warmer feeling between parent and child?
5. Did you notice how the parent in scenario #2 took good care of herself? Why is it important for children to spend some time in another room when they are starting to act nasty?

CHAPTER 4

Our Kids are Hurting and Need to Talk About Difficult Things

WISE WORDS

Wise parents know that their kids may someday choose their nursing home.

This book is mostly about how to take good care of yourself when your kids start arguing and manipulating. This book is also about maintaining life-long, positive relationships with your children. The techniques we discuss are real relationship savers because they enable us to remain calm, loving, and firm in really tough, frustrating situations. When kids feel this type of love from their parents, they tend to copy most things their parents do, and they eventually tend to adopt the same values as their parents. In other words, kids who have strong bonds with kind and responsible parents tend to become kind and responsible people. And, they tend to take good care of us when we turn old and gray! The ultimate key to success is keeping the parent-child bond healthy with lots of listening and heavy doses of empathy.

WISE WORDS

Wise parents know the difference between a manipulating child and one who is hurting and desperately needs them to listen and understand.

Although this book is mostly about dealing with arguing and misbehavior, DON'T FALL INTO THE TRAP OF TREATING EVERY PROBLEM AS AN INSTANCE OF MANIPULATION! Sometimes kids just need someone to listen with a kind, nonjudgmental ear. Sometimes they just need somebody to hear them out and to understand their feelings. More than ever, kids desperately need to know that they can talk to their parents about upsetting, embarrassing, or scary issues. Although it sometimes feels like our kids are trying everything they can to distance themselves from us, it is essential to remember that we continue to be the most important sources of understanding, support, and guidance in their lives. Empathy is the most powerful tool for lessening distance between us and our children, while increasing the odds that they will come to us for guidance.

WISE WORDS

Kids who don't feel listened-to and understood by their parents tend to search for these feelings in other places— in gangs—in cults—in drugs—in sex—etc.

Many parents ask, "How do I talk to my kid about embarrassing or scary things?" or "What do I say when my kid comes and tells me that she's hurting?" The reason talking to kids about difficult issues is so hard is that "talking to" them about these issues is really the wrong thing to do. Instead of talking, try listening! Being able to use the powerful tool of empathy doesn't involve much talking. More than anything, it requires two open ears. Here are three simple steps for using empathy when your child comes to you with a problem:

Three Steps for Using Empathy

1. Listen to what your child is saying and try to imagine how you might feel in the same predicament. Keep your mouth shut during this step.
2. Describe how you think your child might be feeling. Try using a statement such as, "Sounds like you are feeling _____," "This is really _____," or "You must be feeling really _____ right now." Fill in the blanks with the feeling you might experience if you had the problem.
3. Repeat steps 1 and 2 as needed.

Let's take a look at some examples

Example #1: "Nobody likes me."

Child:	Mom, nobody likes me. They all think I'm some type of geek or something.
Parent:	(Imagines how it would feel to have no friends) Sounds like you're feeling pretty lonely at this school.
Child:	Yeah, nobody here ever talks to me at lunch.
Parent:	(Imagines how it would feel to be ignored) That must really hurt.
Child:	Yeah. This school is stupid. I hate it.
Parent:	(Repeats the child's feelings) You hate it.
Child:	I do! (Starts crying)
Parent:	(Imagines what feelings might be behind the tears) You hate it, and it makes you feel really sad.

Child: Nobody understands me.
Parent: Do you feel like I understand?
Child: Yeah.

More important than trying to "fix" the problem, Mom listened and strengthened the bond between her and her daughter by delivering a strong dose of empathy. Often, parents try so hard to solve the problem or give solutions that they forget to lend an open ear.

WISE WORDS
Listening and using empathy is more important than "fixing" the problem.

Let's look at another example:

Example #2: "My friend smokes pot."
Parent: What's up? Is something wrong?
Child: Nothing (but continues to look upset)
Parent: OK—Hey, want to shoot some baskets outside?
Child: OK.
Parent and son go out in the driveway for a one-on-one game of basketball.
Parent: (During the basketball game) You really looked upset today when you got home from school.
Child: I guess. It's Sammy. He's—he's—aw never mind.
Parent: I'm gonna win this time. Watch this move. (Goes for a jump shot)
Child: You think you can beat me? Watch this! (Makes a layup)
Parent: (Still playing the game) I guess Sammy's having some problems?
Child: Yeah. He's—he's—when I saw him this morning, he asked me if I wanted to smoke a joint with him after school.
Parent: (Trying to stay calm) Oh?

Child: I shouldn't have told you.

Parent: (Imagining how his son might feel) You're afraid of getting Sammy in trouble?

Child: Yeah. He's been my best friend since kindergarten.

Parent: (Continues to put himself in his son's place) You don't want to lose your friendship with him.

Child: No.

Parent: What do you think about smoking pot?

Child: I don't want to—I saw what it did to Joel last summer. He's a waste head.

Parent: You don't want that?

Child: No.

Parent: This must be really hard. You don't want to smoke it, but you want to keep Sammy as a friend.

Child: Yeah.

Parent: Thanks for being honest with me. I love you.

Child: What am I supposed to do?

Parent: I don't know. Do you think we should try to get Sammy some help?

Child: Don't tell anybody!

Parent: Do you think keeping this a secret is going to help or hurt Sammy?

Child: I guess—hurt.

Parent: (Trying to understand how hard this is for his son) This is really hard. I'm sorry.

Child: Do you think we can help him?

Parent: (Imagining how his son might feel) You really care about him. We can try.

Child: What are you gonna do?

Parent: I think the first step is making sure that his parents know—so they can get him some help.

Child: This really sucks.

Parent: I hear you. It does! But, maybe we can help Sammy before he really gets hurt.

How did this parent get his son talking about such a difficult topic? First, he locked-in a very strong dose of understanding and empathy. Also, did you notice how he took the boy outside and talked with him as they were playing basketball? A little known trick for getting kids to open up about difficult issues is to talk with them over some other, enjoyable activity. Kids are usually more likely to discuss scary, embarrassing, or frustrating topics if they are doing something besides just sitting with us face-to-face.

WISE WORDS

Kids are usually more likely to talk about difficult issues if they are interacting with us over some other fun activity. Next time your child seems upset, play a game with him, start a woodworking project, or bake some cookies together. You might be surprised what comes out!

Here are some more examples of how a parent might respond in an empathic way. Keep in mind as you read these that THE WAY WE SAY THESE THINGS IS MORE IMPORTANT THAN THE WORDS WE USE! Genuine sadness and caring must come through in our tone of voice and our body language.

Example #3: "Somebody Stole my Bike!"
   Child: Mom! Somebody stole my bike!
   Parent: (In a sad tone) Oh no, I know you really love that bike. This is so sad.

Example #4: "I Hate Algebra."
   Child: I hate algebra. It's stupid!
   Parent: It sounds like you're pretty frustrated with this stuff right now.

Example #5: "I Wish You and Dad Would Stop Fighting."
   Child: I just wish you and Dad would stop fighting all of the time.
   Parent: It's really hard to see us fighting?

Example #6: "I'm fat!"

Child: I hate the way I look. I'm fat—I look like a big
fat whale!

Parent: Oh, sweetheart. You're feeling really sad right now.

All of this listening and empathy is just fine, but don't kids need a little more from us than just an open ear and a bunch of talk about feelings? What happens when kids encounter problems that they don't know how to solve? Don't they need just a little more guidance?

WISE WORDS

Wise parents know how to give guidance while keeping responsibility for the problem squarely on their children's shoulders.

How do we give our children guidance without stealing what they can learn from solving their own problems? Love and Logic offers a five-step process just for this purpose:

Guiding Kids to Solve Their Own Problems

1. Deliver a strong dose of empathy.
2. Place ownership of the problem squarely on the child's shoulders by asking, "What are you going to do about this?"
3. When the child says, "I don't know," we ask, "Would you like to hear what some other kids have tried?"
4. If the child says, "Yes," we give a menu of possible solutions, asking, "How would that work for you?" after describing each option. If the child says, "No," we say, "If you change your mind, I'm here to listen."
5. We give the child encouragement by saying, "Let me know how this works out. Good luck!"

Let's take a look at how the parent from example #1 used this process with her daughter:

Step 1: Locking-in the Empathy

Child: Mom, nobody likes me. They all think I'm some type of geek or something.

Parent: (Imagines how it would feel to have no friends) Sounds like you're feeling pretty lonely at this school.

Child: Yeah, nobody ever talks to me at lunch.

Parent: (Imagines how it would feel to be ignored) That must really hurt.

Child: Yeah. This school is stupid. I hate it.

Parent: (Repeats the child's feelings) You hate it.

Child: I do! (Starts crying)

Parent: (Imagines what feelings might be behind the tears) You hate it, and it makes you feel really sad.

Child: Nobody understands me.

Parent: Do you feel like I understand?

Child: Yeah.

Step 2: Placing Ownership of the Problem on the Child's Shoulders

Parent: What are you going to do?

Child: I don't know. Nothing works—nobody likes me.

Step 3: Asking the Child if He or She Would Like Some Ideas

Parent: Would you like to hear what some kids with this problem have tried?

Child: I guess—yeah.

Step 4: Giving Ideas and Asking, "How Would that Work for You?"

Parent: Some kids decide to make friends with one of the nicer kids by smiling and asking what kind of music or sports they like. How would that work for you?

Child: I don't know. That might work a little.

Parent: Would you like another idea?

Child: I guess.

Parent: Some kids decide to invite one of the nicer kids over to watch a movie or something. How would that work?

Child: I don't know. Maybe.

Parent: Some kids also try to feel better by reminding themselves that it takes some time to make friends at a new school. How would that work?

Child: It takes time?

Parent: Yeah. Sometimes it takes a while before kids make friends at a new school. Do you think it might help to remind yourself of this from time to time?

Child: It makes me feel a little better.

Parent: Thanks for talking. I know this has been real hard.

Step 5: Giving Encouragement

Parent: Let me know how it goes. Good luck!

FOR YOUR THOUGHTS

1. Is it possible that kids are more willing to listen to their parents when their parents listen to them?

2. Loving parents often want to jump in and "fix" the problem when their kids are hurting. Why is this a bad idea? How might this get in the way of really listening and showing that you care?

3. Which of the following would you want to hear from a friend after telling them that you'd gotten a very expensive traffic ticket?

A: "That's outrageous. What you need to do is take it to
court. You can get the fine reduced. Were you really
going that fast? All you need to do is take it to the judge.
That's what I did when it happened to me."

B: "Oh. That's got to be frustrating. I'm feeling for you."

4. What happens to a child's self-esteem when they are allowed
to solve their own problems with guidance? Can you see
how it might go up?"

5. Did you notice how the parents in examples #1 through #6
(pages 19-23) did not discount their child's feelings by saying
something like, "Oh honey. It's going to be all right. Don't
worry." Can you see how saying this could make a child feel
like you are not really listening?

CHAPTER 5

WISE WORDS

*Wise parents know that kids only threaten to starve them-
selves. If this were anything but a hollow threat, there would
be no adults alive today to be tricked by these hollow threats.*

Hearing kids say that they don't want to eat can tug
heavily on a loving parent's heart. We worry about our
kids' physical development. We have concerns about
their health. We develop anxieties about them developing
unhealthy eating habits. And, on top of all of this, we want the

dinner table to be a place of comfort and love. When kids reject our offers of love, through food, loving parents can feel rejected without being aware of it.

There exist a wide variety of myths surrounding childhood nutrition. Each contributes needless anxiety and frustration to our daily lives. Let's take a look at a few of these myths below.

DINNER TABLE MYTH #1
My kids will allow themselves to die of malnutrition if I don't make them eat.

This is not true. Human beings have extremely strong survival instincts. Witness the many reports of people living through unbelievable abuse, depravation, or disasters. We have all heard accounts of people eating such unappetizing items as bugs, spiders, grasshoppers, plants, etc. in order to survive.

Ordinarily the eating issues we deal with while raising kids have to do with personal preference, not life and death. Kids can put up quite a fuss when they would rather have ice cream than vegetables. They understand that parents become emotional around food issues and that kids can often bring parents to their knees by refusing to eat.

Kids have been known to hold their family hostage for hours at the dinner table, simply by refusing to eat. This tactic puts children into a very powerful, but toxic position. Simply stated, this type of power is not good for a kid. It's certainly no good for the parents either! Little by little these kinds of no-win power struggles convince kids that their parents are powerless. Obviously, no good can ever come of this. Wise parents preserve their loving authority by never battling over issues that can't be won.

Parents who check with the pediatricians learn that, in America, it is more likely for a child to die of physical abuse for refusal to eat than to die because he refused the nourishment.

DINNER TABLE MYTH #2
A kid's refusal to eat is a direct challenge to my authority.

A child can only challenge his/her parent's authority when the parent issues orders, such as, "Eat that" or "For crying out loud. There are starving kids in China!" Love and Logic parents know that it is far easier to work with kids when they've been given some small, appropriate choices about food and drink. As we mentioned in the first chapter, control is a basic human emotional need. Parents get more control by giving away little pieces they don't need. And, children who've been given choices have fewer opportunities to really challenge their parents. The choice, "Would you rather have juice or water?" doesn't give a kid the chance to say, "No." In contrast, threatening, "You eat that or else" provides a great chance for a kid to say, "No" and win!

The dinner table is a wonderful place for parents to share control with kids in fun ways.

It's a time when Mom and Dad can give lots of little choices, like:

- Do you want plain bread or toast?
- Do you want mustard or mayo?
- Do you want gravy on your meat or on the side?
- Do you want three green beans or four?
- Do you like what we're serving or would you rather wait until the next meal?

Notice that these choices are very small, and each option the child is given will please the parent. Smart parents never give choices like, "Would you like carrots or candy?" In such cases kids will always choose what we don't like. Instead, Love and Logic parents give choices like, "Would you like to have carrots or celery?" Listed below are some Love and Logic guidelines for giving smart choices:

Guidelines for Giving Smart Choices

1. Never give a choice on issues that might cause a problem for you or anyone else.

2. For each choice, give only two options, each of which is OK with you.
3. If the child doesn't decide in ten seconds, decide for him or her.
4. Give most of your choices when things are going well— before your child gets angry or begins an argument.

The more choices parents give, the easier they find it to boss their kids around when they absolutely need to. That is, control is just like respect. We never have more than we give away. When parents give away plenty of the control they don't need, they are more likely to get the control they really do need. If we give enough choices, and let our children feel a healthy sense of control, we are more likely to be successful when we say, "Wait a minute. I usually let you decide, but I can't do that this time. It's my turn to make the decision. You can choose another time. Thanks for understanding." Parents who frequently play the dictator role, and never allow their kids to make simple choices, can't use this great technique.

Sometimes kids don't want to eat because they simply aren't hungry. This happens to adults. It can happen to kids. Reluctance to eat at this time is not a challenge to authority. It is simply a good decision on the part of the youngster. People who only eat when they are hungry are much better at main-taining an optimum body weight. In fact, force feeding a child who is not hungry may actually damage the child's ability to self-regulate in a healthy way. This may result in an inability to distinguish actual hunger from "emotional" hunger, and can contribute to overeating problems in later years.

DINNER TABLE MYTH #3
A good parent runs the home like a cafeteria.

We once knew a mother who was preparing between three and five different main courses for her family each evening. She said it was because the family members all liked different kinds of foods and they wouldn't eat if she didn't meet their individual needs. Can you imagine the shock in that home when she changed her ways? Can you imagine how much happier she was the day she announced that she was no longer a slave or a cafeteria cook?

This mom announced that everyone would continue to have choices about what they ate, although the choices would be different than in the past. It must have sounded something like this, "Hey guys. There's a lot of peanut butter and jelly in the refrigerator in case you don't like what's served. And, you may just decide to take your money down to Joe's Grill and see if he has anything that suits you better. Whatever you decide will be OK with me."

This mother was only able to do this after several visits with her therapist, who finally helped her to see that she deserved a life of her own—instead of being treated like "kitchen help."

DINNER TABLE MYTH #4
If my kids appreciated how hard I work, they would eat what I serve.

Simply stated, it is entirely possible to appreciate the work of others and still not be hungry or like what is being served. When children are polite but don't eat, it's smart not to get bent out of shape. When children act nasty at the table, it's smart to ask them to leave until they can act sweet.

WISE WORDS
Wise parents know that the battles fought with children about eating eventually become eating disorders after kids leave the family.
(The battles never end. They start out at the conscious level and later move to the subconscious level.)

All of us grew up with very special beliefs and values around the issue of eating. These are deeply embedded in our subconscious levels of thinking. Many of these thoughts serve us well, while some get in the way of rational living. The best way to raise kids who have healthy eating beliefs is to model good eating and to avoid power struggles about food. The best way to raise kids who have unhealthy emotional issues surrounding eating is to model unhealthy beliefs and to turn the dinner table into a battlefield.

Since there is such a wide variety of reasonable values around eating, we're providing more than one scenario in the parent/child dialogues. Pick one that best suits your own value system.

Dialogue #1

Child: I don't want to eat that. You know I don't like turkey.

Parent: (In a gentle, sincere tone) That's what's available. Maybe you'll like what we serve at the next meal better.

Child: But why can't you fix croutons and peanut butter. You know I don't like turkey.

Parent: Turkey is what's available.

Child: But, it's not fair.

Parent: I know, sweetie. Maybe the next meal will be better.

Child: But, you always get to decide.

Parent: I know, sweetie. Maybe you can put in an order for Thursday's meal. Now, do you want to eat the things on your plate that you do like, in a nice way, or would you rather go to your room? Thank you.

Dialogue #2

Child: I don't want that. You know I don't like turkey.

Parent: Maybe you'd rather fix yourself some cold cereal. You decide.

Child: But I want croutons and peanut butter.

Parent: I know. And, what are the choices?

Child: But I don't like the choices.

Parent: I know. And, what are the choices?

Child: You don't love me.
Parent: Nice try, sweetie. Please make your choice or find another place to be while the family enjoys the meal. Thank you.

Dialogue #3

Child: I don't like turkey. I'm not eating that!
Parent: Oh, goody, all the more for the rest of us.
Child: But what's for me?
Parent: Breakfast. We will be serving at 7:30 in the morning.
Child: But I can't wait that long.
Parent: I guess it's turkey or breakfast. You decide.
Child: My friends get to choose what they eat. Monica's mom fixes something different for everybody in the family 'cause she loves her kids.
Parent: Nice try, Pal. Would you rather stay with us or would you rather go somewhere else while we eat? Thank you.

FOR YOUR THOUGHTS

Multiple Choice Questions:
Pick the answers that have a high probability of being correct. (It is possible to find more than one right answer for some of these questions.)

1. A child who refuses to eat
    a. will die from malnutrition
    b. may crave attention more than food at the moment
    c. may enjoy watching his/her parents beg and threaten
    d. should be force-fed if necessary
    e. is rejecting the love of the parent who provides the food
    f. can go without eating for several meals without suffering any permanent health problems
    g. should sit at the table until he/she eats
    h. may be luring parents into a battle that is not worth winning

If you chose answers "b" "c" "f" and "h" you're right on track with Love and Logic!

2. What happens when parents issue commands that they cannot actually enforce like, "Eat that!" What happens to the parent's authority when the child realizes that the parent cannot actually make them eat?

CHAPTER 6

WISE WORDS
Wise parents don't allow words to gain shock value.

What can be more upsetting than hearing a choice four-letter word flow from the once sweet and once innocent lips of your own flesh and blood? When our children use words that would shock the most seasoned sailor, isn't it tempting to give their mouth a thorough wash and rinse? And isn't it also tempting to give them one of the good old-fashioned swearing lectures? "Don't you use that language!" "Watch your mouth!" "You get a civil tongue in your mouth, young lady!" "I didn't raise you to have a trash mouth like that."

Why do kids swear when they know how angry and upset it makes us? Why? Because some know exactly how angry and upset it makes us! Kids generally do things for only one or two reasons. First, they do things to get what they want or to avoid having to do something unpleasant. Secondly, if they aren't successful with this, they will do something else just to get some excitement, attention, and feelings of control. When things don't go their way, swearing can start an exciting and entertaining parental show of frustration and anger—like no other technique!

Lectures and threats make the problem worse. In fact, the best recipe for getting your kids to swear around you reads something like this:

How to Make Swearing a Bigger Problem in Your Home
1. Show surprise and shock when your child uses a bad word.
2. Get really mad and yell.
3. Lecture them about how bad the word is.

Why do kids swear more around parents who do these three things? Because they quickly learn that if you really want to push Mom or Dad's "buttons," just use one of these great little "button-pushing" words! Swearing then becomes the treatment of choice for punishing your parents for doing something you didn't like, steering your parents away from the real issue when you might be in trouble for something else, or just getting some attention when things get dull.

WISE WORDS
Lectures and threats make the problem worse. Wise parents take the fun out of swearing by encouraging the use of the "dirty" word in some other place.

Encourage our children to swear? What kind of book is this? This is a book about parenting today's modern version of child. The old kid models—those produced a generation or two ago—worked a bit differently. In the "good old days" kids could be operated via remote control. Parents could tell kids what to do—or what not to do—and kids pretty much did what they were told. Why? Kids could be controlled by their parents externally because society basically said, "Your parents know best. Listen to them." The remote control models are a thing of the past. The "modern child" is now bombarded on a daily basis with messages from TV shows, movies, advertising, music, and peers. These messages generally say, "Parents are dumb, they don't know what they are talking about, and you don't really have to listen to them because they really can't make you do anything you don't want to." Today's parents have a much more challenging job than parents a generation or two ago: Teaching kids to follow healthy internal controls without the use of anger, lectures, threats, or warnings.

How do we help kids learn to control themselves from within? One strategy is to give them the skills to figure out when and where it is OK to do certain things—and when and where it is not. Swearing is a great example. While saying, "Clean-up that mouth of yours!" usually has less than satisfactory long-term results, saying something like, "That's a great word for expressing your feelings, honey—but only when nobody else can hear it" avoids an argument and has better chances of long-term success. One parent we know handled a swearing episode like this:

Child: I hate this *&%$#* chore.
Father: I know. That's a great word for saying how you feel—as long as nobody else hears it. Say it as much as you want to—in your room, outside, in the bathroom—anywhere nobody else has to hear it.
Child: Well, I hate this *&%$#* chore.
Father: Will you take that word someplace else?
Child: Why should I?

Father: I'm just thinking that something very sad might happen if you don't.

Child: Well, I hate doing this stupid job!

Father: I know—and thanks for listening.

Child: What are you gonna do if I don't do this stuff?

Father: (In a very soft and sad tone of voice) That would be so sad. I guess I'd have to hire someone to do it and pay them with money from your savings. What a drag.

Child: You can't do that.

Father: (Walking away) I love you too much to argue about this—try not to worry about it.

By avoiding an argument over whether or not the word was "dirty" and encouraging his son to use the word someplace else, this father achieved a number of very important things:

1 Saying, "*&%$#*" did not become a way for his son to get attention, entertainment, or control.
2. Saying, "*&%$#*" did not become a way for the boy to punish his father.
3. This dad avoided a control battle with his son and preserved their relationship.
4. This father's attention didn't get diverted from the real issue—the chores!
5. This kid is beginning to learn that being angry or frustrated is OK—as long as you don't use hurtful or offensive language around others.

What's a parent to say or do if their child continues to use nasty language? What can we do if our kid knows to "take it someplace else" but doesn't? Choose the option you think is best:

What should a parent do if their child insists on swearing around them? (Pick the answer you think fits best with Love and Logic.)

a. Pay some kidnappers to take him.
b. Encourage him to play in the middle of a busy street.
c. Move to another state without telling him.
d. Say, "This is so sad. You said that word around me again. What an energy drain! I'm going to have to do something about this, but not now. Try not to worry about it."

If you circled option "d" you're right on target with Love and Logic! If you chose options "a" through "c," you may need a little "brush-up" on the basic concepts.

WISE WORDS
When kids insist on swearing around their parents, their parents fall back on the "energy drain" principle: Swearing drains energy from the family, but there's nothing like your kids cleaning the toilets or staying home from the amusement park to charge it up!

When kids know to "take it someplace else" but choose not to, wise parents help them shape-up by using a two-step process. The first step involves buying yourself some time so that you can put together a plan—and keep your kid wondering (or hopefully worrying) about what you are going to do. Here's an example of this first step in action

Child: *&%&$#$#*@!
Parent: (Whispering) Oh no. This is sad. You said that word around me again. What an energy drain! I'm going to have to do something about this—but not now—later. Try not to worry about it.
Child: What are you gonna do?
Parent: (Still with a whisper) Try not to worry about it. Maybe you'll have some idea for fixing the problem before I have to. I'll get back to you later.

After avoiding the power struggle, this parent took a couple days to make sure that:

1. Both she and the child had calmed down.
2. She had a fool-proof "energy pay-back plan" that involved one of the following:
   a. Having the child do a chore to repay her for the "energy drain" of listening to the word.
   b. Having the child pay for a babysitter while the rest of the family "recharges" on a fun outing.
   c. Having the child pay someone else to do a chore around the house.
   d. "Resting" instead of taking the child someplace he or she really wants to go.
3. She had practiced delivering the consequence with sadness instead of anger or sarcasm.
4. She was prepared to handle how upset the kid was going to get when she described the "energy pay-back plan."
5. She was prepared to take one of the child's favorite possessions until he was willing to "restore the energy."

Here's how the second step might unfold:

Parent: Have you decided what you are going to do to repay me for the energy drain we talked about?
Child: What energy drain?
Parent: Remember when you swore the other day, and I said that I was going to get back to you about it?
Child: Yeah. So what do you want me to do about it?
Parent: (With sincere empathy) I know this is hard. What do you think?
Child: (Shrugging shoulders) I don't know.
Parent: Would you like some ideas?
Child: I guess...whatever.
Parent: Some kids decide not to do anything. How would that work for you?
Child: (Sarcastically) Good idea.

Parent: (Still with empathy) Oh, that would be so sad. Because, then I would have to think of something on my own—and I might think of something pretty hard for you to do.

Child: Well what am I supposed to do?

Parent: Some kids decide to do some of their parent's chores to pay them back for the energy drain. How would that work for you?

Child: I don't want to.

Parent: No problem. If you get something done by tomorrow night, then I'll know that you decided to fix this on your own. If not, then I'll think of something.

Child: (Angry) What?

Parent: (In a very sincere tone while walking away) I don't know. Try not to worry about it.

Now let's consider two possible scenarios: One in which the child decides to fix the problem on his or her own, and one where the parent must deliver a consequence:

Scenario #1: Child Decides to Fix the Problem

Parent: I noticed that you cleaned the garage. I sure do appreciate your help.

Child: It's stupid that I have to do that stuff just 'cause I used a word you think is dirty.

Parent: I know—but thanks for the help.

Scenario #2: Child Decides Not to Fix the Problem

Child: Dad! Who's that outside?

Parent: Oh, that's a kid down the street who I've paid to help out in the yard. Let me know whether you would like to pay him directly or need me to take some money out of your band trip savings. You decide.

Child: (Very angry) What? Why are you so mean?

Parent: I noticed that you hadn't gotten anything done to repay me for the energy drain, so, rather than fight

with you about it, I decided to hire Johnny to give
me a chance to get some rest.

Child: I hate you!

Parent: I'm sorry you feel that way. I still love you.

Child: Well, this sucks! I'm gonna go live with my friends.

Parent: (Walking away) I'll be happy to listen to you when
your voice is calm like mine.

FOR YOUR THOUGHTS

1. How fruitful is it to argue with a child about whether a
   word is "dirty" or not?
2. What does a Love and Logic parent do instead?
3. Parents can use the "energy drain" approach if their kids will
   not take their swearing elsewhere. Can you see this approach
   working with other irritating behaviors like lying, temper
   tantrums, misbehavior in public, sibling bickering, etc.?
4. Who has the power when parents try to respond with a
   consequence when they are frustrated, angry, or caught
   off guard? Who has the power when parents delay the
   consequence instead of trying to respond immediately?
5. When parents delay the consequence, what are they modeling?
   Is it possible that they might be showing kids that it's smart
   to calm down first and think—before reacting?

CHAPTER 7

I'm the only kid in school who doesn't have them! They're only $200.00.

Those would look great on you. I'll contribute $50.00 and you can pay the rest.

WISE WORDS
Saying "No" to a $200 pair of sneakers does not constitute child abuse.

Almost everyone hates to feel "different" from the crowd. In today's age of high tech toys and designer clothes, it can be very easy for kids to feel left out of the loop if they don't have what others do. When they bring these frustrations home, and when they begin to ask for things we don't believe they should have—or things we can't afford in the first place—it's easy to get sucked into either giving in or arguing back and forth about the issue.

Often our own fears about being excluded or rejected are triggered. Most parents can remember times from their own childhood when they felt excluded, rejected, or different. This makes it even harder to stay objective when our kids say things like, "I know these sneakers cost $200, but I'm the only kid at school that doesn't have them." Sometimes our hearts ache at the very thought of our kids having to go through some of the same pain we experienced as children. As we remember this personal pain, it can be very easy to leap off the cliff of good judgment.

LEAPING OFF THE CLIFF OF GOOD JUDGMENT

Path Number One

Parents tend to follow one of two different paths as they leap off the cliff of good judgment. The first is an attempt to convince the child he/she doesn't have to be just like everyone else. This is known as the, "If your friends jumped off the roof, would you have to do it too?" tack. It usually takes the form of either a lecture or an argument.

Child:	Dad, I really need those Intergalactic Space Sneakers. They're only $149.95. We have to go to the store this weekend for sure or they'll be out of them. All the other kids have them already.
Dad:	You don't need those. Your shoes are almost new.
Child:	But Dad. All the other kids have them.
Dad:	Don't give me that. They don't all have them. And besides, why do you have to be like everyone else. I suppose if your friends jumped off the cliff, you'd have to do the same thing?
Child:	It's not like that, Dad. My shoes aren't cool. I can't look like a dork. I told you I didn't want those stupid shoes in the first place. Why can't you ever let

| | me have what I really want instead of the stuff you think is so great? |

Dad: Look, young man, you don't have to be just like everyone else. Why can't you have a little pride in being able to think for yourself for a change? What am I raising, a follower who can only do what everyone else does first? How many times have we had this talk? I'm getting tired of your constant begging and being dissatisfied with the things we give you. I work hard to give you the best and you never appreciate it. Well, it's time for you to show a little appreciation for a change.

Child: I knew it! I knew it! You don't care. You don't understand. I hate you!

Dad: That's enough of that. You're grounded!

How sad for both father and son! This parent is tricking himself into thinking that the situation is settled. Dad may be thinking that if the kid is grounded often enough, or if he gets enough stern lectures, he will figure out who is running this house.

Yeah right! We all know that what we just witnessed is a LOSE-LOSE situation. The relationship between Dad and the child has been dented once more. And most kids don't give up that easy when someone tells them they don't need something. The long term results of Dad's lecturing and grounding will merely be more and more resentment, disrespect, and manipulation.

It's very likely that the problem will rear its ugly head again before long. The power struggle has really only just begun. There is a good chance that Dad will be approached a week later with:

Child: Dad. You can't trust anybody over at that school. Someone stole my sneakers. I put them in my locker so I'd have them for gym class, but when I went to get them they were gone.

Dad: Well, did you lock your locker?

Child: Sure, Dad. Do you think I'm stupid? You always think it's my fault. There's a bunch of kids who can open any of those stupid, cheap locks the school gives you to use. It's not my fault. And I've got to get some new sneakers. I can't go to gym class wearing my boots.

Dad: Well, did you report it to the principal?

Child: Yeah, but he never does anything. He doesn't care. When are we going to get some new sneakers, Huh? And don't forget. I want those Intergalactic Space Sneakers this time.

Dad: We're not buying any new shoes until I've had a good talk with those school people. Just leave me alone and let me figure this out.

It's easy to see that this problem is a long way from being solved. Unfortunately, Dad got himself in over his head by trying to argue with his boy and trying to convince him that he didn't need Intergalactic Space Sneakers.

Path Number Two
The second path parents tend to follow is that of giving in to the demands of the child as a way to avoid unpleasantness. Effective parents believe that it's fun to give their children things, and they believe that giving is a good thing. They also know that the correct time to give is when their children are not begging or demanding. Giving things to demanding kids is about as distasteful as giving a kiss to someone who says, "Give me a kiss right now, dammit!"

WISE WORDS
*Never expect that giving concessions will bring gratitude.
Concessions made to demanding kids rob them of
the opportunity to learn respectfulness, responsibility,
and how to earn what they want.*

Love and Logic parents know that self-confidence is born out of struggle and accomplishment. They understand the value of kids earning what they get. They also know that kids grow in healthy ways each time they struggle and work hard to achieve one of their goals. A kid who has a goal of wearing Intergalactic Space Sneakers might just be willing to work toward owning them if the parent stays cool, doesn't lecture, and doesn't give in.

Let's listen in to a Love and Logic parent who understands the value of the "matching funds" approach to solving these types of problems.

Child: Dad, I really want a pair of those Intergalactic Space Sneakers. All the other kids have them already, and they only cost $149.95.

Dad: I think that's a great goal. I'd like to see you wearing them!

Child: When are we going to get them. We'd better hurry. The store will be out of them if we don't hurry.

Dad: I can contribute $49.95. As soon as you have the rest we can go buy a pair.

Child: But I don't have the rest!

Dad: I know. It's hard not having enough money. What are you going to do?

Child: But Dad. That's mean!

Dad: I know. It's hard not having enough money.

Child: But where am I supposed to get the money?

Dad: I don't know. A smart kid like you will probably figure it out. I hope it all works out for you. I'd love to see you wearing those shoes!

The kid in this scenario provided a wonderful opportunity for his father to fall into a deadly trap. The door to this trap was opened when the child said, "Well, where am I supposed to get the money?" At this important point, the direction of the conversation could have easily turned into an argument if Dad had fallen into the trap of lecturing or getting angry. Let's see where this discussion might have gone if Dad had not remembered to stay away from giving orders.

Child:	But where am I supposed to get the money?
Dad:	Get a job.
Child:	There aren't any jobs.
Dad:	Of course there are. You have to go out and knock on some doors.
Child:	But nobody's going to give me a job. All the old people in this neighborhood hate teenagers anyway.
Dad:	Now you know that's not true. You've met them all at the block party and they were real nice to you.
Child:	Oh, sure, Dad. They were good then 'cause you were there and they were trying to impress you. Besides, how am I supposed to keep up my grades if you're making me work all the time?

Is there even a slight chance that the most persuasive parent could convince this youngster that jobs are available? Of course not! The availability of jobs isn't the issue. What is the real issue? Winning the argument is what the kid really cares about! Notice that as the son exhausted the value of arguing over the job, he moved on to the issue of grades. At the Love and Logic Institute, we refer to this kid strategy as "diversionary warfare." This common game involves getting your parents to argue over some side issues so that they don't have time and energy to effectively deal with the real one.

Who knows what bird walk this kid will take Dad on next? We all know that Junior is not suddenly going to sit up straight and say, "Oh, Dad. I just realized something! You're right and I'm wrong."

WISE WORDS
To avoid a fight with your kids, tell them what you will provide, not what they have to do.

FOR YOUR THOUGHTS

1. Are children amazingly good at picking up on the pain and insecurities their parents experienced as kids? Might it be more difficult to avoid giving in to demands for $149 sneakers if you felt excluded from the group or "different" as a kid? Will some kids use this to manipulate their parents?
2. Which kids turn into the most responsible and productive citizens? Ones who are given everything they want? Are those who learn to struggle and work for what they desire better off in the long run?
3. Why do wise parents avoid saying things like, "You don't need that"?
4. Why did the parent on page 47 say, "I don't know" when his son asked, "But where am I supposed to get the money?"
5. Are kids forced to think and solve their own problems when parents say, "I don't know" instead of giving lectures?

CHAPTER 8

WISE WORDS

*The best person to answer the question "but why?" is
the person asking it. Wise parents respond to "But why?"
with "And why do you think?"*

A whiney "but why?" can grate on one's parental nerves
like few other sounds coming from the mouths of
babes. The first time it flows from their lips, it seems
almost harmless. But like small drops of water during water
torture, each repetition gets more and more irritating. As our

child counters every bit of parental wisdom with these two little words, most of us finally feel like yelling, "BECAUSE I SAID SO! THAT'S WHY!"

Children tend to ask "Why?" for three reasons:
1. They are curious and honestly want to learn about something.
2. They are actually complaining or saying, "I just want you to know that I hate this and don't understand why I can't have my way."
3. They are trying to manipulate their parents by using "But why?" as a form of verbal "brain drain," hoping that the parent will either give in or give them an entertaining sideshow of parental frustration and anger.

WISE WORDS
Wise parents recognize the difference between genuine curiosity and manipulation.

When kids are genuinely curious about matters in their life, most parents notice that "Why?" has no manipulative, whiney ring to it. When a parent feels good about answering a question, and the child is being sweet, this is a great time to have a fun conversation. Most parents live for these warm times, when their kids ask funny questions like, "Daddy, why is your hair gone on top? Where did it go?" And most parents want to be as fair as possible in answering all of their children's questions. Enjoy these wonderful times!

Unfortunately, sometimes our desire to answer all of their questions leads us down the wrong path when our kids are complaining or turning on the manipulation. A common misconception among many parents and mental health "experts" is that when kids ask a whiney "Why?" we must always provide a lengthy explanation, consisting of all reasons why we have set a limit or imposed a consequence. In other words, the parent must provide psychotherapy each time they discipline their children.

"BUT WHY?" MYTH #1

*Kids always need lengthy explanations of why their parents
have set limits or delivered consequences. Otherwise, they
won't learn anything and will be forever resentful.*

A LOVE AND LOGIC TRUTH

*Don't fall into the trap of giving your child long explanations
every time you set a limit or give a consequence.
It typically contributes more to a child's brain development
if he or she has to spend time thinking about the answer—
rather than immediately receiving it from the parent.*

Lengthy explanations make the problem worse for a number
of reasons:

1. They reinforce or encourage manipulative behavior by giving
   it undue attention.
2. They force the parent into doing more thinking than the child.
3. They sap essential (and often very rare) parental energy.
4. They allow the child to gain control and get an entertaining
   show of frustration from the adult.
5. They damage the parent-child relationship.

Let's take a look at how a well-meaning parent can make the
problem worse:

Child: I want a new Super Fast Wheels Race Car.
Parent: That's the one you broke the other day when you
         got mad. I'm not buying you another one. If I keep
         buying you things every time you break something,
         you're never going to learn how to take care of your
         things. I'm doing this because I love you, sweetheart.
Child: (With a whiney voice) But why won't you buy
         me one?
Parent: I know it's hard for you to understand. If I buy you
         something new every time you break something,

you won't learn how expensive things are, and you won't know that money doesn't grow on trees. I just want you to be responsible. You just can't have everything you want in life. Life doesn't work that way. Sometimes you just have to accept the consequences of things you have done.

Child: But why?

Parent: In the real world people are going to hold you responsible for your mistakes. They aren't going to give you a free ride. I know it's hard, but life isn't easy. Your daddy and I have to work hard for things. If Grandma gave Daddy everything he wanted, would he know how to work for a living? I don't think so.

Child: But why?

Parent: Your daddy has to do a lot of work that he doesn't really like, but he does it anyway. He has to pay for things when they break, so he is more careful with them. Do you see Mommy and Daddy throwing our things at the wall? No. We have to pay for them with our own money if we break them.

Child: But why?

Parent: (Exhausted) Why don't you understand? How many times do I have to explain this to you? Things in life aren't free! We have to work hard for what we have. I'm not buying you that car!

Child: But why?

Parent: (Beyond frustrated) Because I said so! You're not getting that car. Forget about it!

Child: (Even whinier) But why can't I have it?

Parent: (Swatting the child on the bottom) Go to your room!

Child: (In the room breaking more toys)

Where do you suppose this child learned to raise her mother's blood pressure so effectively? A quick peek at the way very young kids think can help us understand how this nasty habit might get started—and how to keep it from driving us nuts with our older kids. Preschoolers say what they think and think what they say. In other words, one way they learn about the world is by talking and wondering out loud about their day-to-day experiences. Many experts believe that this "thinking out loud" is essential for learning how to solve problems and getting along with others. As our children grow and learn, usually their thinking begins to spend more time inside their heads rather than flowing from their lips. Soon, a voice develops within to guide their actions.

When our preschooler feels angry or frustrated, it is very natural for them to wonder out loud, "But why?" in a very whiney way. To every young parent's regret, it is also very common for this "But why?" to repeat five, ten, or fifteen times. When we ignore this behavior or encourage our child to take it someplace where we can't hear it, he or she will soon learn that the best place for a whiney "But why?" is within one's own head.

In contrast, when parents respond with anger and frustration, kids soon learn that saying "But why?" is one way to gain attention, excitement, and control in their homes. As the parent's face gets redder and redder, the young child sits back and seems to think, "Wow! Look at this! I'm just a little kid, but look how powerful I can be! What a show!" With this unfortunate turn of events the very natural and curious wondering out loud becomes the complaining and manipulative "But why?" every parent dreads. Let's take a look at how a Love and Logic parent might handle the same situation:

Child: I want a new Super Fast Wheels Race Car.
Parent: (In a sincere, sad tone of voice) It's really sad when you get mad and break your own things. What are you going to do?
Child: Buy me a new one. Please!
Parent: Maybe you can do enough chores around here to earn a new one.
Child: But why won't you buy me one?
Parent: (In a sweet tone of voice) And why do you think?

Child:	But why?
Parent:	And why do you think?
Child:	But why?
Parent:	(Smiling and walking away) And why do you think?
Child:	(With a frown and both hands on her hips) I don't want to think! I want you to think!
Parent:	(Still walking away) If you haven't figured it out by tomorrow, I'll talk with you then. Maybe some time in your room will help you think easier?

The next day

Child:	Why won't you buy me a new car?
Parent:	Why do you think?
Child:	(Looking at the ground) 'Cause I threw it?
Parent:	You are such a good thinker. You figured it out all by yourself!
Child:	How many jobs do I have to do to get one?

This mother did some very powerful things that helped her remain calm and allowed her child to gain wisdom rather than unhealthy attention and control:

1. She avoided lengthy explanations for the limit she set.
2. She handed the problem back by saying, "What are you going to do?"
3. She provided a healthy dose of sadness and empathy rather than anger and frustration.
4. She took good care of herself so she wasn't tempted to say "'Cause I said so. That's why!"

WISE WORDS

Wise parents know an angry, "'Cause I said so!" makes life for them and their children a whole lot worse.

Anger and frustration also breed resentment and revenge. When children hear something like, "'Cause I said so!" the parent-child relationship suffers. When this relationship suffers, many children soon become teenagers who resort to retaliation in the form of rebellion. These tactics include refusing to do chores, doing them in a sloppy way, picking friends that the parent dislikes, coming home late, using disrespectful language, lying, poor grades, drugs, sex, etc.

When children hear their parents issue angry commands, they also develop a voice inside their heads that says, "I'm not smart enough to make my own decisions." And "When I make poor decisions, other people get really mad." The focus of their concern falls on what others think of them rather than how much pain a poor decision might cause them personally. They spend the rest of their lives trying to avoid making decisions and trying to keep their friends happy. When faced with life and death choices about drugs, alcohol, driving, and sex, these teenagers and young adults fall prey to peer pressure. They reason, "Even though they've been drinking, I better ride with my friends. Otherwise they might get mad." Instead of, "If I ride with my drunken friends tonight, I might die. No thanks! I'll take my own car."

Here's how a parent we knew used some Love and Logic techniques with his teenager:

Teen: Why are you so old-fashioned? Why can't I have beer at my party?

Parent: (Smiling) Why do you think?

Teen: This sucks.

Parent: (In a sincere, sad tone) I know.

Teen: But why are you being so strict? I'm gonna be 18 in two months. Don't you know 18-year-olds can drink beer in this state?

Parent: I know.

Teen: Then why?

Parent: Because it's illegal.

Teen: You're so old-fashioned. Why can't you just bend the law a bit?

Parent: (Walking away) I guess that's for you to figure out. I love you too much to fight with you about this.

By the way, I call the police when I'm aware of underage drinking taking place.

Even in Love and Logic homes, kids experiment with trying to get their own way. There is nothing wrong with this. What is wrong is for them to get what they want through manipulation and arguing. Here's another Love and Logic example of handling a child who decides to experiment with the "But Why?" game.

Kid: Mom. I really need a TV of my own. All my friends have them. They get to watch their own shows without bothering everybody else.

Parent: I bet that would be great. You might want to do that when you have your own home.

Kid: But I need it now. It won't do any good to have it then. That's stupid.

Parent: I know.

Kid: But why?

Parent: What do you think?

Kid: But why won't you tell me?

Parent: What do you think?

Kid: But that's what you say all the time.

Parent: (In a calm yet firm tone) I know. By the way, my energy is being drained right now. And you know what has to happen when my energy gets drained.

Kid: Oh, sure. Then I have to do some of your crummy housework. Just forget it! You're so selfish!

Parent: I know.

WISE WORDS

Love and Logic parents become more like a cloud than a brick wall in the face of attacks or arguments.

When under attack we have a couple of choices. One choice is to become like a brick wall. We are tough and immovable.

When someone throws a rock at a brick wall, the brick wall does not crumble. However, when the rock bounces off it leaves a scar. The person who threw the rock can always revisit the wall and think, "See. That's the damage I did."

A cloud is very different. When a rock is thrown its way, the rock disappears. What happened to the rock becomes a mystery to the thrower. The person who threw the rock can revisit the cloud but can't see any damage and always has to wonder, "I wonder what happened to that rock?"

As you revisit the last discussion Mom had with her daughter about the TV, you can see that Mom behaved more like a cloud than a brick wall. When her daughter said, "That's stupid!" the words appeared to have no effect. They more or less disappeared. Mom calmly said, "I know" and continued to state her position.

WISE WORDS
Parents who try to be the "brick wall" soon have and feel many battle scars.

FOR YOUR THOUGHTS

1. When was the last time someone played the "Why Game" with you?
   a. How well did that person react to your providing facts and good reasons?
   b. How frustrated did you feel while it was happening?
   c. How did you feel after it was over?
   d. Is your relationship with that person better now than before the situation?
2. What rule of Love and Logic do we violate when we allow ourselves to be sucked into the "Why Game?" (See pages xxiv-xxv for these two rules.)
3. Do you know someone who likes to play the "Why Game?"
   a. Would this be a good person to practice your new skills on?

   b. How would you feel if you came out on top with some-
     one who plays the "Why Game?"
4. The parent on page 57 set a firm limit with his teen about no
   underage drinking. Why is a loving parent willing to call the
   police when they find that their child has violated the law?
5. Do you know any parents who actually buy alcohol for
   their teen's underage drinking parties? Does this make you
   as sad—and mad—as it makes us?

••••••♥••••••

CHAPTER 9

Disrespectful Looks and Actions
(The Nonverbal Barbs)

Can you see your brains when you roll your eyes like that?

WISE WORDS

Wise parents don't allow themselves to be drawn into arguments over their kids' body language.

Don't kids sometimes give us the darndest looks when things don't go their way, or when they think we're being "unfair?" When their eyes travel to the backs of their skulls, isn't it hard not to say, "Don't you roll your eyes at me! You look at me when I'm talking!" When we're in the middle of some serious discipline, and a smile creeps onto our child's face, isn't it almost automatic to say something like, "You think this is funny? You'll wipe that smile off your face if you know what's good for you!"

NASTY LOOK MYTH #1

*When our kids give us disrespectful looks, they
need a good old fashioned "talking-to!"*

DO NOT FALL INTO THIS TRAP! Although a good old fashioned "talking-to" might make us feel better temporarily, all of the attention, anger, and frustration we show in the process just teaches our children that such behavior is a credible way of dealing with problems. In other words, lectures and threats actually make the problem worse!

WISE WORDS

*The more we lecture, threaten, and yell about nasty looks,
the more our children learn that nonverbal barbs are
an effective way of controlling others and getting an
entertaining show of frustration and anger.*

Experimenting with nonverbal barbs or "hooks" is a very normal part of growing up. Helping kids learn to use healthier ways of communicating and solving problems requires that parents do three things:

Three Steps For Teaching Kids that Nasty Looks and Actions Don't Pay
1. Minimize the anger and frustration your children can "pull" from. Try using humor or encouraging the behavior.
2. If your child does what you want, don't make a big issue out of the looks he or she transmits.
3. If your child refuses to do what you ask, teach in a very calm and loving way, that this behavior makes it harder for you to do the nice things you often do for them. In other words, show your child that nasty looks and defiance backfire.

STEP ONE:
Minimizing your anger and frustration

WISE WORDS
Never let a manipulating child see you sweat.

When our children see us handling nasty behavior with humor instead of anger they reason on the subconscious level, "Wow! I tried everything to make my mom mad, but she still handled me without breaking a sweat! She really loves me! She's really strong. I guess I must be OK after all!" In contrast, when kids see their parents using frustration and anger, they begin to reason something completely different and less healthy, "Uh oh. My mom can't control me. Maybe she's weak? Maybe she just doesn't care about me? I must be a pretty hopeless case if she can't make me behave."

When parents avoid getting sucked into lectures and arguments by their kids' nonverbal hooks, their children eventually learn that the "evil eye" really doesn't work. In other words, when we stay calm, ignore the behavior until we can deal with it calmly, or smile and say something like, "That's a pretty good mad face, but I bet you can do better," it takes all of the fun out of being nasty. The true benefit of this approach is that our kids get to see us handling them in a calm and loving way. A parent we met years ago described how he really got creative. When he'd see his daughter's eyes beginning to roll, he'd put a real surprised look on his face and ask, "Wow! Can you see your brains when you do that?" The kid would stomp away, trying to look mad. Apparently she couldn't keep it up for long. Soon he'd see her trying to hide a smile.

Let's take a look at how to have some fun with nasty looks:

Parent: Bill, I need to tell you something, and I think it will be good if you roll your eyes, give me a dirty look, or just say, "Not fair!"
Child: You're weird.

Parent: I know. Yesterday, when I had to pick you up at school because of your fighting, I burned up a lot of time and energy.

Child: (Irritated) What?

Parent: Well, I just don't think I have the energy to take you camping this weekend like we had planned. I'm just too tired-out from dealing with your problems at school.

Child: (With a nasty look) Unfair!

Parent: Oh, I'm glad you have those looks and words to help you feel better about this. This is really tough.

Child: But it's not fair!

Parent: (In a calm tone while walking away) Do you think saying that is going to make me change my mind?

Child: (Sarcastically) Yes, I do. Come on!

Parent: (Giggling) The thing I love about you is your sense of humor.

Step two:
Don't fight over nasty looks if your child does what you want.

Have you ever seen a kid give you a dirty look but do what you asked anyway? How's a parent to respond? Choose the solution you think might work the best:

a. Say, "Don't give me that attitude! When I was a kid, I had to chop wood with my bare hands. We couldn't afford an axe. Back then it snowed all year round, too! Had to stand out in the cold without any shoes. Kids these days don't know how good they have it!"

b. Say, "You show a little respect around here, young man! Don't you give me that look! Look at me when I'm talking! Wipe that smile off your face!"

c. Say, "Thank you."

If you picked option "c" you are right on track with Love and Logic, and your kids will probably continue to do most of the things you ask of them. Why? Because they know you appreciate it when they do. If you chose option "a" you might feel better for a little while, but your kids will probably make fun of you behind your back. Finally, if you chose "b" you just shot yourself in the foot! When we focus on the dirty looks, instead of the fact that our kids are actually doing what we want, they soon feel unappreciated, resentful, and less willing to do things for us.

WISE WORDS

It's simple. Don't fight with your kids over nasty looks if they are actually doing what you want! Just say, "I know you don't like this, but thanks for doing it for me anyway. I love you."

Here's how a Love and Logic parent would handle this type of situation:

Parent: Will you help me with the dishes, sweetheart?

Child: (Rolling eyes and making faces) I hate doing the dishes. I hate it.

Parent: (In a soft tone of voice and smiling) I know you hate it. Sometimes I do too. But, will you do this just for me? Thanks.

Child: (Making faces but helping parent with the chore) I hate this job. I think it's stupid to have to do it. I should be doing my homework right now.

Parent: Thanks for doing this even though you hate it. Your help really means a lot to me. Thanks! I love you, sweetheart.

Child: Yeah. But I still hate this job.

Parent: (Smiling) Yeah, but you really helped out anyway. Thanks.

STEP THREE:
If your child refuses to do what you ask, teach them that nasty looks and actions can backfire.

WISE WORDS
Wise parents don't do special things for kids who treat them like barnyard waste.

When I (Charles) was about ten years old, I took my slingshot, aimed it skillfully at the side of our metal barn, fired with precision, and watched with disbelief—and pain—as the rock bounced back and nailed me on the forehead! Talk about natural consequences! Kids desperately need to learn that "shooting" nasty looks at others is like shooting rocks at a metal barn—something pretty unpleasant usually bounces back your way. In today's world, people have actually been killed for looking at the wrong person in the wrong way. Understanding the effects of being defiant and broadcasting nasty looks is an essential survival skill!

Healthy parents can help their kids learn this valuable lesson by waiting until their child wants them to do something special and saying with genuine love and empathy:

"Oh, this is sad. I do special things for people who treat me nice. Maybe next time."

How will most kids respond to this piece of parental wisdom? Will they thank us for it? Of course not! Most kids worth keeping will blow a gasket! And, many kids will plead, beg, yell, deliver a stinging guilt-trip, and eventually slam their bedroom doors behind them.

A COMMON PARENTING MYTH
If a child's behavior immediately gets worse after using a technique, the technique isn't working.

A LOVE AND LOGIC TRUTH
If a child's behavior immediately gets worse after using a technique, the technique IS PROBABLY WORKING!

DON'T STOP EFFECTIVE TECHNIQUES JUST BECAUSE YOUR KID THROWS A FIT! This is one of the most destructive things a parent can do, because it teaches children the following very unhealthy lesson: "If my parents try something I don't like, all I have to do is get a little nastier. Then they'll back down! I guess the way you get the things you want in life is by being nasty."

WISE WORDS

When you use an effective technique, be thankful when your kids get mad and throw fits. This is how you will know your approach is working. Stick with it! In the long run, you'll be glad you did!

In the long run, families are always happier and healthier when parents stick with Love and Logic, even when their kids temporarily rebel. Let's take a look at how one parent used these techniques to deal with her son's defiance and nasty nonverbal behavior.

Parent: Steven, I was wondering if you could help me clean up the yard on Saturday.

Teen: (Rolls eyes and mumbles something under his breath)

Parent: Will you help me, please?

Teen: This is stupid. Why do I always have to do this stupid work around here?

Parent: Am I asking you nicely?

Teen: I got stuff to do. (Twists face into a nasty scowl)

Parent: I know you don't want to do this, but will you do it anyway? Will you do it just for me?

Teen: (Walks out of the house, slamming the door behind him)

Parent: (In a sad tone of voice) This is really sad. I'll get back to you later. Try not to worry.

Saturday comes and goes without Steven lifting a finger to help with the yard. As a result, his mother silently goes on strike. By Tuesday morning he's also starting to run out of clean clothes, there's not a speck of his junk food left in the cupboards, Mom hasn't cooked him a hot meal for three days, and he's starting to wonder what's going on. Here's how their next conversation unfolded:

Teen: (Peeking into the refrigerator) Mom, when are you gonna go shopping? There's none of my stuff around here.

Parent: (In a very gentle, sincere tone) Oh, this is sad. I do special things for people who treat me nice. Maybe when you start helping me out more.

Teen: (Very angry face) What are you talking about?

Parent: Remember when I asked you very nicely to help me with the yard? It was really sad when you just walked away and then didn't help me.

Teen: (Rolling his eyes)

Parent: (Still in a gentle sincere voice) Have you noticed that when you refuse to help me with things—and when you give me those dirty looks—it makes it a lot harder for me to do the nice things I usually do for you?

Teen: Well, I don't care.

Parent: Oh what a relief. Now both of us are happy.

Teen: But, you need to go to the store.

Parent: I'll be happy to buy you the things you want when I start getting more help from you.

Teen: But, but—it's against the law not to buy your kids food.

Parent: I know. That's why I put all those vegetables and Spam in the fridge.

Teen: (Walking away in a huff)

Parent: I know you're really mad, so it would probably be a good idea if you stormed out of the house and slammed the door really hard. Make sure you slam it hard.

Teen: (Thinking, "If she thinks I'm gonna slam that door, she's got another thing coming!")

FOR YOUR THOUGHTS

1. Have you ever noticed how a child's eyes glaze over as you give a lengthy lecture?
2. Have you ever met an adult who relied mostly on nasty looks to manipulate and "punish" other people? How much fun is it to be around such people?
3. Why does encouraging an irritating behavior often make it stop? Might it be because strong-willed kids typically don't like to do what other people want?
4. Is it more likely that your child's behavior will get better— or more likely that it will get worse—immediately after starting these techniques?
5. What do you say to yourself if your child throws a fit when you use Love and Logic? For a hint, turn to page 66.

·······♥·······

CHAPTER 10

WISE WORDS
*Wise parents encourage their kids to go first class
on their own money.*

wealthy businessman gave his teenage son a ride to
school each day. It was a chance for them to have some
time together, and the school was on the way to Dad's
office. The route they took passed the local Chevrolet dealer.
It became a habit for the teen to point out the Corvettes in the
showroom window with the comment, "Dad, that's what I

want when I'm sixteen. That's the coolest car in town."

Dad would respond each time with, "That's great. I bet any kid would love a car like that." This short conversation gradually became a ritual that appeared to be enjoyed by both.

On the boy's sixteenth birthday, the friendly banter changed when the teen said, "Dad, I'm sixteen now. It's time for you to buy me that Corvette. I need it by next Saturday. I promised my girlfriend that I'd take her to the game, and she's expecting me to drive a Corvette. I went in and talked to the salesman. He's a nice guy and he said that we could come in on Friday and he'd give us a great deal."

"Where did you get the idea I was going to buy you that car?"

"Well, you told me a bunch of times that you thought that was a good car. Every time I told you that I wanted it, you agreed. Besides, lots of dads with less money than you buy their kids cars for their sixteenth birthday."

"I agreed that it was a great car, and I agreed that any kid would love to have that kind of a car. I never said that I would buy it for you. It would probably be too expensive for you. Have you got enough money to own a car like that?"

"Dad, we can afford that car. We're rich!"

"Oh, Pal, you're confused. I'm rich. You might be rich someday, too, if you're willing to work as hard as I have. In the meantime, I'll be glad to let you drive my car when I'm not going to need it. You'll need to make a deposit into my savings account equal to the insurance deductible so that if you have an accident the car can get fixed right away. And you will need to get your share of the car insurance paid before you drive."

"Oh, great! How much is that going to cost me?"

"I really don't know, but that's why we have an insurance agent. He can bring you up to speed on those kinds of expenses. Why don't you give him a call."

WISE WORDS

Never give a kid the bad news about the cost of something, if someone else will do it for you. Why? Children, like adults, are always angriest with the messenger.

This wise father knew several important concepts about kids and driving:

1. Kids who have to work hard to earn their cars and related expenses are usually safer drivers than those who don't.
2. Kids need to learn about the cost of driving. They can do this a little at a time by starting out with the insurance costs.
3. Parents who provide "life on a silver platter" greatly reduce a youngster's ambition and personal drive to succeed on his/her own.
4. Driving is not a right. It is an opportunity and a privilege.

Returning to our story, the son did not give up on his dream of being the proud driver of a shiny new Corvette. He launched into an argument with his dad and gave it a good try.

"But, Dad. You don't want me to go back on my promise to Allison do you? You always tell me my word has to be good. Now I have to look like a liar just because you decide to be selfish." (Casting bait, hoping his dad will take the bait and go for the argument. There is still a chance if Dad will argue about the son's honesty—or his own selfishness.)

Dad chose to sidestep this invitation to argue by responding, "Yes, that looks like a problem. What are you going to do?"

"I guess you or Mom will have to drive me around if you're going to treat me like a baby. I'll be the only kid at our school who can't have a car. How am I going to look? Geez!"

Getting angrier and angrier, the teen tried a scatter gun attack on Dad. "I'm a good kid. I do my homework. How am I supposed to earn money and get good grades? You don't want me to get bad grades do you? Besides, I'm not like those other jerks at school on drugs and stuff. You don't understand! You don't care! All you care about is making my life hard and treating me like a baby! Geez!!!"

Even though this was very difficult, Dad stayed calm. He knew that allowing his son to get his way through the use of anger, arguing, and manipulation would only encourage him to try this approach more and more. Dad also understood that it requires much more love to "hold the line" in a calm way than to give in.

Dad countered his son's verbal brain drain with, "I'm sorry this isn't working out the way you planned it. You have some choices. You can pay your insurance and drive my car. You have the choice of buying a car you can afford, or you have the choice of finding some other ways to get around. Let me know what you decide. We'll talk about this again."

They arrived at school. Without even saying goodbye, the boy slammed the car door and was off. We're sure this father felt terrible.

WISE WORDS
Doing the right thing for your kids often feels terrible at the time.
The results and good feelings come much later.

FOR YOUR THOUGHTS

1. Is it quite probable that this teenager will look back at age thirty and think, "Boy my dad made me mad at times, but he loved me and he sure taught me how to be responsible. Thank goodness!"
2. Why does it sometimes take thirty years before our kids are thankful for the discipline we provide?
3. Do you know any parents who are unwilling to wait that long? Do you know any who try to buy thankfulness from their kids by giving them everything they want? Have you noticed how this never works?
4. Why is it dangerous for parents to pay for their teenager's cars? Are kids more careful with things they have earned themselves?
5. Would you rather have your teen mad at the insurance agent or you?

CHAPTER 11

Why don't you like any of my friends?

I've been wrong trying to boss you around about friends.

WISE WORDS

Wise parents know that strong family relationships and good parenting are far more powerful and longer lasting influences than peer pressure.

What's a parent to say when their kids show up with friends that look more like something from the late night horror show than the sweet children we wish they'd play with? What's a parent to do when their children's friends have more tattoos than a room full of Hell's Angels and more metal in their noses, ears, lips, and other parts of their bodies than the Bionic Man? Most parents really worry about what types of friends their kids "hang out with," and it's clear that our children's peers can have a very powerful influence on their lives.

Are you ready for the good news? Despite all of the power other kids can have over our children, we are still the most influential people in their lives! When parents have strong, positive relationships with their kids, and help them learn to make wise choices, kids usually end up pretty responsible and pretty happy—even if some of their friends are "responsibility challenged."

Ready for some more good news? If we establish a strong bond with our kids, and don't destroy the relationship we have with them by fighting about things we really can't control— like who they chose as friends—they end up being more like us than they want to be! Yes! Despite their valiant attempts during adolescence to be completely different than their parents, kids who love and respect their parents eventually wake up at approximately age thirty, look in the mirror, scream, and say, "Oh my God! I'm just like my mom!" We call this the "U" of Parental Influence. As shown on the next page, parents generally enjoy a high level of influence over their young children. Have you ever noticed how toddlers tend to copy almost everything their parents do and say? As our children get older they start to look more to their peers as a source of influence. This shift is typically the most extreme during early adolescence. This is the time when many parents wonder whether aliens have abducted their "real" kids and replaced them with ones that look like them but act completely different. Young adults who received good parenting as kids once again begin to see their parents' wisdom. I (Charles) remember reaching this point and thinking, "Geez, Mom and Dad weren't that dumb after all!"

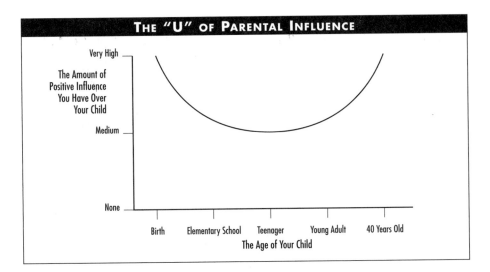

THE "U" OF PARENTAL INFLUENCE

Unfortunately, many well-meaning parents unintentionally force their kids to make poor decisions about friends. They do this by trying to control who their children like and spend time with. How does this happen? Let's take a look at an example of how a parent might fall into this trap with a teenage girl

Parent: I noticed you've been spending a lot of time with Randy.

Child: So?

Parent: I heard that he's been getting himself in a lot of trouble at school. I don't think he's the type of kid you really want to be spending time with.

Child: What's wrong with him?

Parent: I told you. He's always in trouble. Why do you want to spend time with kids like him when there are so many really nice kids right here in the neighborhood?

Child: He's cool. Why don't you like any of my friends?

Parent: It's not that I don't like him, but he's not the kind of kid I want you spending time with.

Child: You can't tell me who my friends should be!

Parent: Don't you talk to me in that tone of voice, young lady! If I catch you spending time with this boy, you're grounded! I mean it!

Child: (Rolls her eyes at Mom)
Parent: Don't you roll your eyes at me! You look at me
           when I'm talking! I'm doing this because I love you!
Child: (Under her breath) Yeah right.

What has Mom just done? She's just shot herself in the foot by making Randy even MORE attractive to her daughter! When we fall into power struggles with our kids over their friends, our kids begin to reason, "Mom and Dad can't tell me what to do! I'll show them!" As a result, we force our children into spending extra time with the kids we like the very least— just to prove to us that they can! When parents damage the relationship in this way, their influence is permanently weakened. Instead of eventually adopting values very similar to their parents, children of over-controlling parents spend a lifetime making poor decisions in an attempt to prove to their parents that they won't be controlled. These kids spend their lives doing anything they can (including drugs, joining gangs, dropping out of college, marrying someone who beats them, piercing their eyebrows, etc.) to prove that they are not like their parents.

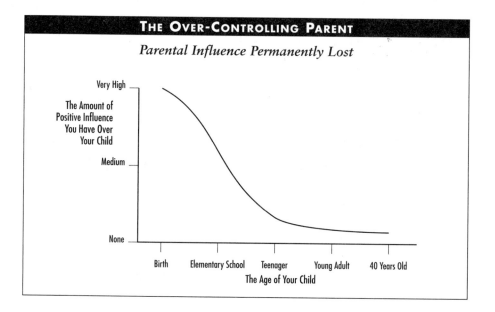

THE OVER-CONTROLLING PARENT

Parental Influence Permanently Lost

WISE WORDS
Parents who battle with their kids over friendship choices create teenagers who sneak around behind their backs.

Don't fall into the trap of trying to control who your children choose for friends! Smart parents realize that they will never win at this game. Instead, they do a number of things to raise the odds that their kids will make good decisions when their friends do not. In other words, smart parents help their kids develop a voice inside of their heads that asks, "I wonder how my next decision is going to affect me?" instead of, "What can I do so my parents don't find out about this?" Below are some tips to help your kids make wise decisions—even when their friends are not:

TIP #1:
Avoid power struggles over friendship issues.
A positive and honest parent-child relationship is by far the most powerful tool for helping kids resist negative peer pressure. When children know they can talk to their parents about their friends without being lectured or yelled-at, they are more likely to adopt their parent's values and ask them for help when their friends start making poor choices. Here is how one father built a bond of trust by replacing lectures with a strong dose of empathy:

Parent: I heard that your friend Ron got in some trouble over at the grocery store.

Child: Oh great! Here it comes.

Parent: What?

Child: Here comes the lecture on how I should get some "nice" friends.

Parent: What are you talking about?

Child: You aren't going to tell me not to be friends with him?

Parent:	No. I decided that I have been wrong trying to boss you around about your friends. Mostly, I was just feeling sad for him. It must be pretty scary to get caught for shoplifting.
Child:	I don't think he really did it.
Parent:	I'm just glad you aren't having to go through all of that—talking to the police, hiring your own lawyer, going to court. That's scary.
Child:	Yeah.
Parent:	I know it must be hard for you to see him going through this. Hang in there.

The parent in this example just took a huge step toward bolstering his influence. The more we listen and the less we lecture, the more powerful we become! Did you also notice how this parent subtly implanted information about having to go to court and hiring one's OWN lawyer?

TIP #2:
**Send positive messages about your child's ability
to resist negative peer pressure.**
Parents shoot themselves in the foot when they infer that something "bad" about a friend might rub off on their child. Many well-meaning parents unintentionally set their kids up for failure by saying things like, "Don't you spend time with that boy. He's up to no good," or "If you hang around with that bunch of friends, you're going to find yourself in a whole lot of trouble!" Lectures like these send a very clear, powerful, and dangerous message to our kids: "You are a really wimpy kid! You can't think for yourself, and you can't make wise choices when your friends aren't. You are a follower rather than a leader."

Messages like these are powerfully dangerous because our kids tend to pick up on them and live them out. In fact, research clearly shows that kids generally behave in ways that confirm the expectations of adults around them. When we expect the worst, we tend to get the worst. Thankfully, kids also tend to act in ways that confirm our positive expectations! When parents send positive messages about their children's ability to resist peer pressure, the odds for responsible behavior significantly increase. Here's an example:

Parent: Sally is really lucky to have a friend like you!

Child: What are you talking about?

Parent: Well, I heard that she got caught with some drugs at school. What a drag.

Child: How did you hear?

Parent: It's amazing how fast word travels in a town like this.

Child: So?

Parent: I'm just glad she has at least one really good kid like you as a friend. Maybe some of your smart thinking will rub off on her.

Child: (Too shocked to talk)

Parent: I'm just glad you make smarter choices than what she did. She must really be hurting.

Child: Yeah.

Parent: I'm glad you are the kind of kid who can make smart decisions even when your friends aren't. I love you. Give me a hug.

Tip #3:
Give your kids a way of saying "no" to their friends without looking like a nerd.

Peer pressure is powerful because it feeds on the basic human emotional need to feel included and accepted by one's peers. Teenagers often find themselves in a horrible bind. That is, if they say "No" to drugs or other unwise choices, they look like a wimp in the eyes of their friends. At the same time, if they say "Yes" they suffer life and death consequences. When parents encourage their teens (and younger children as well) to use them as an excuse for saying "No" it can really help. Here's an example to clarify what we mean here:

Parent: It can be pretty hard being a teenager these days.
Child: Yeah.
Parent: With all the drugs and gangs and all the other tough decisions.
Child: Yeah, lots of kids at school are doing speed and other stuff.
Parent: It must be hard when they ask you to join in. Would you like an idea about what you might say to them so they won't think you are a nerd?
Child: What?
Parent: If somebody you like starts wanting you to do something you don't think is smart you might say, "Last time I did something like that, my dad almost killed me. Man, he's got friends all over this town. He's got the worst temper! He finds out about everything!"
Child: (Giggling) You wouldn't kill me—would you?
Parent: (Smiling) Naw, I'd spare your life. But if your friends think I'm real tough, they might give you a little more slack for saying "No."
Child: Yeah, they might even feel sorry for me.

TIP #4:
Make your house an inviting place for your children and their friends.

The healthiest, happiest, and safest teenagers we have known had parents that extended a warm welcome to all of their children's friends. In many of these families, the family home actually became a gathering place for these friends. Although the carpets and furniture tend to take a beating, and the noise level can get a bit high, homes like these become safe places where children and teenagers can maintain strong family bonds while enjoying the company of their friends. When we encourage our kids to bring their friends over, and their friends end up enjoying it, our kids tend to spend more time at home where we know what they are doing. Kids tend to get in less trouble at home with their parents than on the streets with their friends! Smart parents provide a friendly, supervised place with high expectations and appropriate limits for the behavior of their own children and their friends.

One of the most fatal errors is to make your home a place where neither your child nor his or her friends feels comfortable or welcome. Many children and teens in this country feel alienated from their homes because their parents extend a less than warm and fuzzy welcome when their friends come to visit. One parent I (Charles) knew used to say to his son, "Forget about bringing those good-for-nothing kids into this house!" Is it any wonder that his son spent most of the time away from home? Is it any wonder that his son spent most of his time with the very friend his dad hated the most? And, is it any wonder that his son and this friend spent most of their time together doing exactly the opposite of what his father would have approved?

WISE WORDS
One of the most powerful things you can do is to get your kids' friends to fall in love with you.

Every time you see one of your child's friends, smile, shake their hand, and say something like, "I'm glad you came to visit" or "It's really nice to see you!" Also, try to notice something positive about the friend and say something like, "I noticed you got a new bike!" This greeting is more important than it might seem. When we shake hands, smile, and say something nice, we start to develop a positive emotional bond with our children's friends. This bond is powerful because it ultimately draws this child AND your own closer to you, and it reduces the chances that they will be compelled to rebel against your authority.

Tip #5:
Involve your teenager in setting a reasonable curfew.
How many battles have taken place between parents and their teens over curfews? Of all the potential hazards of parenting a

teenager, this issue seems to fall right at the top. Although parents may not be able to control who their kids choose as friends, they can and must have a say in where and how late they "hang-out" with these friends. Teens with parents who are able to set and enforce reasonable curfews feel more loved and generally get in a lot less trouble than kids with parents who can't. And, kids who have some degree of choice in selecting the curfew times are usually more likely to follow them! The following example provides some ideas for involving your teen in the process. Notice how this parent starts with an earlier time than actually desired and then shares control by allowing his daughter to choose between two somewhat later times.

Parent:	How about if we make your curfew eight o'clock?
Teen:	Aw man! Julie doesn't get off work until nine. I won't get a chance to hang out with anybody.
Parent:	You think you need more time?
Teen:	Yeah. How about eleven? That way I can see Julie, and we can go over to Brandon's.
Parent:	I guess eight o'clock doesn't give you enough time. Sorry. Let's make it either nine-thirty or ten. You decide.
Teen:	But I think eleven would be better.
Parent:	I know, but I'm just the kind of parent that worries. I guess it's 'cause I love you so much. You decide— either nine-thirty or ten.
Teen:	Ten
Parent:	OK. I hope you have a great time. I think I will sleep better if I set my alarm for ten. Just shut it off when you get home. That way, I will know not to start worrying unless it goes off.
Teen:	(Rolling her eyes) Whatever.
Parent:	Just leave me a note with the names and phone numbers of the people you will be with. That way, I can get you help real fast if something happens to the car or you run into any other sort of trouble.
Teen:	What happens if I'm late and I can't help it?

Parent: No problem. Just call me and let me know where you are and that you will be home very soon. I will set the alarm for a little more time. I promise not to be mad or yell. I just want to make sure you are safe. I love you.

TIP #6:
Enforce the curfew at all costs.
Smart parents delay the consequence. That is, when their teens end up coming home at 12:45 a.m. instead of 10:00 p.m., they just look at the kid and say, "I was so worried. I'm so glad you are here."

Not until they've put together a solid plan do they deliver a consequence. Here's how a parent we met handled this problem with his teenage daughter:

Teen: (Walks in the door at 12:45 a.m.)
Parent: (In a sincere, sad tone of voice) Oh—I'm so glad you are OK. I was worried sick. Thank goodness you are home. Give me a hug.
Teen: Me and Ray were talking, and we just lost track of time.
Parent: The most important thing is that you are OK.
Teen: You're not mad?
Parent: (Calmly but very firmly) I'm so mad I can't see straight. I'm going to have to do something about all of the worry you caused for me. But I'm not going to do anything until I think about it for a while. Get some sleep—try not to worry about it.
Teen: What are you going to do?
Parent: (Whispering) I don't know. It will be fair. Try not to worry about it tonight.
The next day
Teen: (Calls her father at work) I can't believe you put a lock on the steering wheel! I'm late for school, and it's all your fault. Come home and take it off!
Parent: I'll be happy to take the lock off of your steering

wheel when I know that I won't have to worry about you coming home late. I'll see you after work.

Teen: This sucks! (Hangs up)

A week later:

Parent: (Takes lock off of wheel)

Teen: I can't believe you did that Dad! If you really loved me you wouldn't make such a big deal out of this curfew.

Parent: I'm sorry you feel that way. I took the lock off because I know that tonight you will be home by ten.

Teen: You can't tell me what to do!

Parent: I know. But I think you will make a wise choice. I love you too much to argue.

Teen: (Gets in the car and drives off)

There is a happy ending to this story. Dad stayed up and waited for his daughter. About 9:45 that night he peeked out the window to see her car pull into the driveway. Describing this to us, he laughed and said, "She's such a strong-willed kid. The funniest thing happened. I watched her shivering in the cold outside the door for fifteen minutes before coming in. She kept pacing back and forth in the snow, looking at her watch, probably thinking, 'I'll walk through this door on time but not one bit early!'" What's the best part of this father's story? His daughter never betrayed her curfew again and has become a responsible adult who's fun to be around.

FOR YOUR THOUGHTS

1. How wise is it to say, "Don't you spend time with those kids. They're going to get you in a world of trouble"?
2. When we criticize our children's friends, might we also be criticizing our child?
3. How do teenagers of over-controlling parents deal with peer

pressure? Do they make lots of wise decisions, or do they make lots of poor ones just to prove that they have more control than their parents?

4. The parent on page 85 said, "I'm so mad I can't see straight. I'm going to have to do something about all of the worry you caused for me. But I'm not going to do anything until I think about it for a while." Why is it important for kids to know that sometimes their behavior makes us mad? Did you notice how Dad expressed this anger without yelling or belittling his daughter?

5. What's smarter? Trying to control who our kids spend time with? Or teaching our kids to make wise choices even when their friends don't?

CHAPTER 12

WISE WORDS

Parents are wise to worry about the type of "education"
their kids are getting on the Internet.

W e've opened the door to a new visitor in our homes. As our kids sit down at the computer, get "online" and start "surfing the Web," this visitor walks into our lives for either good or evil. Most people would think it ludicrous to invite a stranger off the street into their home— and leave this person alone with their kids in their bedroom!

Even more unthinkable would be to invite a stranger who
might bring profanity, pornography, or bomb-making advice!

While no sane parent would leave their kids alone with
this type of person, many parents think nothing of allowing
their children to interact unsupervised with information on
the Internet that may prove nearly as harmful. Simply stated,
kids are never any healthier than what they see and hear on
a daily basis.

Wait a minute! Computers and the Internet have tremendous
potential for improving our lives! And, the vast majority of
information on the Web ranges from harmless to incredibly
helpful. That's the problem! If the Internet were purely evil,
we'd have no indecision or debate about the issue. We'd do
whatever we could to keep our kids away from it! But, this is
NOT a simple, black and white issue. While the potential for
danger is very real, the potential for benefit is tremendous.
And, some kids handle any negative information they fall upon
without negative effects, whereas others seem to gravitate to it,
get hooked, and become destructive.

Some children are very quick to take advantage of the
indecision their parents have about this issue, and they create
masterful arguments when their parents try to set limits on
computer or Internet use. Knowing what limits to set can be
difficult. On one hand we want to protect our kids from the
negatives of the Internet. On the other hand, we don't want
to deprive them of its benefits. Notice how the child below
takes advantage of his parent's indecision.

Parent: You are spending way too much time on the
Internet. Look at this phone bill!

Child: Well, not all of that time is mine. You and Mom
use it too!

Parent: We do. But you've been spending hours in your
room every evening glued to that computer. That's
going to stop. One hour a day is enough. That's it.

Child: Not fair! Why do you guys get to use it for as long
as you want?

Parent:	We pay for it young man. That's why.
Child:	Oh, so I guess you just don't care how I do in school.
Parent:	What?
Child:	Back when you and Mom were in school, you did all your homework with books. Kids these days need the Internet. How am I supposed to keep up with my friends at school if I can only use the computer for an hour?
Parent:	You haven't been spending all of that time on homework. I know it.
Child:	You just don't understand. I have. School is a lot more demanding than it was when you were a kid. You just want me to fail.
Parent:	No we don't. We want the best for you.
Child:	Then why are you making it impossible for me to do good in school?
Parent:	OK, then how much time do you need?
Child:	Four hours a night at the very least.
Parent:	What? No way. Three hours is the max—now I mean it!

What's a parent to say or do when their kids say such things? Clearly, we need a plan for this new and challenging issue. Understanding some of the potential dangers of the Web is the first step.

DANGER #1:
Access to harmful information
Never before in history have kids had greater access to information. Have you ever heard the sayings, "Information equals power?" and "Power corrupts?" Unfortunately, too many children are repeatedly exposed to information about sex, violence, and defiance of authority figures before they have the maturity to handle these messages responsibly. Power without maturity is obviously a very dangerous thing!

In years gone by, parents were the gatekeepers of information in the family. When information was judged inappropriate for children, parents had a much greater ability to withhold this information or shield their children from it. As a result, most kids were not bombarded with violent or sexualized information. And, kids were not constantly exposed to messages saying, "Don't listen to your dumb parents. Don't listen to your dumb teachers. If they were cool they'd get off your back."

Too many kids have more power in the home than their parents. They know more about pornography, drugs, rock and roll, hate groups, bomb making, violence, and other exciting topics than their parents. Is it any surprise, then, that so many kids today have little or no respect for adults?

DANGER #2:
Potential for secrecy

How many stories do we hear about kids getting hooked into inappropriate or downright dangerous activities via the Internet, without their parents even having a clue? There is no substitute for good parental supervision. But, this supervision is tougher than ever because of the potential for secrecy computers and the Internet provide. Children can go online and get off-track without leaving the house.

DANGER #3:
Potential for addiction

Mom trudged into my (Charles') office, plopped down in a chair, took a deep breath, and lamented, "He just sits there hour after hour in front of that screen. He's like a zombi—just fixated on that thing. I can't get him away from it, and he gets so nasty when I interrupt him! We can hardly pay the bills he runs up! I've tried everything. Nothing works!"

In typical therapist form, I questioned, "How long has this been a problem for your son?"

"Oh, my son? I was talking about my husband! Well, little Sammy is almost as bad. He comes home from school, throws his coat in the corner, and slams his bedroom door behind him. That's all I see of him unless there's a power outage, his hard disk crashes, or he's arguing with his dad over whose turn it is to use the phone line."

It doesn't take long to find someone who knows a computer "junkie." Sadly, people who live with one see problems similar to those created by drug, alcohol, or gambling addictions.

People get addicted to the Internet, for the same reasons people get hooked on gambling. At the heart of this addiction is what psychologist-types call a "variable-ratio schedule of reinforcement." What? To understand this simple concept with a complicated name, it's easiest to imagine yourself at the helm of slot machine in Vegas. Dunk a quarter in that sucker, pull the handle, watch the dials spin—nothing. Dunk another quarter—pull the handle—still nothing. Dunk, dunk, dunk—nothing. Dunk another quarter and whamo—the bells ring, the lights flash. You are a winner! Your mind starts racing, "Maybe if I try again, I'll hit it even bigger! This is a lucky machine!" Here goes another quarter—nothing. Another—nothing. Another—nothing. Another—nothing. Another—nothing. Another—nothing. You start to reason, "The next one's got to be the big winner! It's got to be!"

Slot machines are addictive because one never knows when they will pay off, and it's pretty tempting to start believing that the next try will be the winner. Unfortunately, the "next try" usually leads to many more "next tries"—and fewer and fewer coins in the pocket. The term "variable-ratio schedule of rein-forcement" simply means that the number of attempts required to get a payoff or "reinforcer" varies in an unpredictable fash-ion. The machine pays off just enough to keep people believing that the next try will be a winner, but not enough, in most cases, to keep them from losing their shirts!

Now imagine yourself surfing the Net. One search—nothing very interesting or exciting. The next—still nothing. The next—nothing. One more—whamo! Like gambling, people get hooked on the Internet because it pays-off just like a slot machine. Users start to believe that just one more search—the next one—will be the one with the "information jackpot." Unlike slot machines, coins don't fall out of a computer's disk drive. Instead, "winning" means access to information that helps the user feel strong, intelligent, loved, excited, or aroused. Some people get hooked into fulfilling these needs via a computer screen rather than through healthy human relationships and activities. The symptoms they display are very similar to those of alcoholics, compulsive gamblers, and other types of addicts. These include:

1. Excessive use of the substance or activity, despite the following negative consequences:
    a. Loss of friendships and damaged family relationships
    b. Serious financial difficulties
    c. Loss of job or very poor school performance
    d. Association with dangerous people
2. Serious irritability or anger when restricted from the substance or activity.
3. Denial regarding how dependent they have become on the substance or activity.

DANGER #4:
Potential for damaging family relationships
This section is probably best left short and simple. In too many homes across this great land of ours, people spend more time paying attention to electronic devices than each other. Too many arguments take place between family members over these devices, and too many quiet, loving family moments have been traded in for a chance to see the latest sitcom or to explore the vast expanse of "cyberland."

WISE WORDS
There are no things more powerful than quiet, loving, or silly moments between us and our kids. These moments can only flower when the distractions and temptations of our TVs and computer screens are switched off. Try experimenting with a TV-free and computer-free weekend. You may be pleasantly surprised!

Are you ready for some practical solutions for making the Internet friend rather than foe? The approach we recommend depends largely on the child. Some kids seem to be born easy going. They do most everything we ask of them, and they can be trusted with a relatively large degree of responsibility. I have a friend with a kid like this. When her child was six, he told her that his favorite superhero was "cool" but really shouldn't fight so much. He continued, "It's bad that he fights 'cause some kids might see that made-up fighting on TV and do it at school 'cause they think it's real." Kids like this really do exist—right here on Earth! And, these are the children who tend to make wise choices even when they see or hear negative things on radio, television, or computers. Below are some tips for parents of typically respectful and responsible kids:

Internet Tips for Parents of Typically Respectful and Responsible Kids
- Place the computer in a family area, instead of the child's room.
- Have honest discussions and send positive expectations.
- Set a reasonable time limit on daily computer use.
- Expect the child to pay for any use over the time limit.

Place the computer in a family area, instead of the child's room. There is no substitute for good parental supervision! Placing the computer in a family area like the kitchen, dining room, or living room can significantly cut down on your child's temptation to surf the less desirable portions of the Web. It's also a whole lot easier to drop in on them from time to time, look over their shoulder, and say, "This looks pretty interesting! What are you working on?" Children often protest this type of involvement, but the underlying message they receive from it is very positive and comforting: "Kid, I love you enough to set some limits, and I love you enough to be interested in your life." Here's how a parent might talk to a child about moving the computer out of his or her room:

Parent:	Joe, I'd feel better if the computer were in the family room instead of in your room.
Child:	Why?
Parent:	I like to be with you, and I enjoy seeing what you are working on.
Child:	But I like having it in my room.
Parent:	I know. I can understand that.
Child:	Can I keep it in there? Please?
Parent:	I want it out here. Thanks for understanding.
Child:	This is dumb.
Parent:	I know.
Child:	But this isn't fair.
Parent:	I know. I love you too much to argue.

Have honest discussions and send positive expectations.
Honesty is almost always the best policy with our kids. Some well-meaning parents shy away from talking with their kids about sensitive issues. Some worry that the discussion will scare their kids. Others fear that talking about dangerous or harmful things will actually encourage their kids to try them. A very interesting phenomenon takes place when parents worry in such ways. Psychologists and educators call it the "self-fulfilling prophesy." When parents worry that their kids cannot handle certain types of important information, their kids often read this in their parents' nonverbal behavior. Research has clearly shown that our attitudes, fears, and beliefs tend to "leak" out of us non-verbally. In fact, between 60% and over 80% of what we communicate we do without words! Solid research has also shown us that kids are fabulous leak detectors and decoders! When kids pick-up on our worries that they are weak, they tend to behave in weak ways. Ironically, their behavior tends to match our greatest fears!

WISE WORDS
Without saying a word, we constantly show our kids what we believe they can be. They will either live up to our highest expectations—or down to our greatest fears.

DO NOT nag or lecture your child about the woes of the Internet! Typically this makes the problem worse by creating a power struggle. Once the struggle begins, your child will be forced to make poor decisions just to "win" the battle.

A more productive approach involves merely sharing information in a factual way and communicating that you believe your child will make wise choices. In the following example, notice how the parent sends "strength-messages" rather than "weakness messages."

Parent: Isn't the Internet great?
Child: Yeah.
Parent: Some of the things you can learn are great. Do you think there are also some things on it that aren't so great?
Child: What?
Parent: I've read that there are Internet sites that have really bad things having to do with hating other people, sex, and other pretty serious things. I've also read that some kids get hooked by this stuff and start doing really horrible things.
Child: Yeah? But I don't look at those.
Parent: I know! That's the great thing about you. One of the things I love about you is that you make smart decisions about those serious things.
Child: What do you mean?
Parent: (Parent puts loving hand on child's back) I know you are the kind of kid who knows not to get hooked into looking at the bad stuff on the Net. I'm so proud of you. Give me a hug.

Set a reasonable time limit on daily computer use.
Simply put, kids should not be spending hours each day surfing the Net, watching television, or playing video games! For most kids on most days, one hour is more than enough time to spend engaged in these activities. This DOES NOT mean one hour of computer plus one hour of TV plus one hour of video games!

Setting a time limit on these devices will not win you any popularity awards with your kids. Some may even consider this a violation of their constitutional rights. Let's take a look at how one father set this limit and dealt with his daughter's reaction:

Parent: Feel free to use the computer for up to one hour per night.

Child: What? An hour? That's too short! Why?

Parent: (With great excitement) I just read that kid's brains grow best when they are doing things other than watching TV, playing video games, or using the computer. There is research showing this! It is really interesting!

Child: That's dumb.

Parent: (Grinning) What? So you aren't impressed by this research?

Child: (Rolling her eyes in great disgust) No Dad. You are sooo weird.

Parent: (Still smiling) That's what your mom says, too.

Child: But I need more than an hour.

Parent: There is one option. You could call the Internet company and find out how much each minute of service costs. I will pay for the first hour—you can pay for any extra time.

Child: (Going for a second eye-rolling) Goll!

Parent: I know it's hard. Thanks for understanding.

Expect the child to pay for any use over the time limit.
What's a parent to do if their kids go over the daily time limit? Exceptions to this time limit can and should be made when your children need to complete more lengthy school assignments. Otherwise, kids need to be held accountable for exceeding this limit by being expected to pay for excess use. Of course, there are a number of convenient payment options available. Some kids pay with extra chores. Others pay with money they have saved. And others pay with possessions. Here's an example.

Notice how the mother locks-in a strong dose of empathy before delivering the consequence.

Parent: (In a sincere, sad tone) What a bummer. (Long pause)
Child: What did I do?
Parent: This is so sad (Another long pause)
Child: Whatever happened, I didn't do it.
Parent: What a bummer. Last week you were on the Internet five hours longer than you were allowed.
Child: But—but—but.
Parent: How are you going to pay me for these extra hours?
Child: I don't have any money.
Parent: No problem. You can pay with chores or toys. Let me know by tomorrow what you decide.

Some Thoughts on Electronic Limiting and Monitoring Devices
Products are available which claim to make it very difficult for your kids to access harmful information via the Internet. None of these devices are foolproof. None of them teach your child self-control. Our friend Dr. Foster Cline often comments that wise parents realize that their children's first girlfriends or boyfriends will not come with electronic safeguards, designed to limit any potentially harmful information or activity. We add that their first cars won't have these safeguards either. Might it be unwise to rely on these devices at the expense of teaching children how to limit their own behavior? How is this teaching done? By modeling wise decision-making, having honest discussions with your kids, and allowing them to experience the consequences of their mistakes at a young age.

Internet Tips for Parents of Very Challenging Kids
Many kids aren't quite as easy to deal with as the ones in the examples above! These are the children who really challenge our sanity and need a much different approach when it comes to TV, the Internet, and video games. The tips provided above will not be sufficient for extremely strong-willed kids or children

with emotional or behavioral difficulties. For a variety of reasons, some kids require much greater patience, more hugs, tighter limits, more consistent consequences, and more extensive supervision. Some children are born with difficult temperaments, whereas others develop problems as a result of being overindulged, neglected, abused, or exposed to chaotic environments. Television, the Internet, and other popular media tend to have a much greater negative influence on children with these problems. These are the children who tend to gravitate to and mimic violent and otherwise inappropriate content. One parent made this comment, "I can't seem to keep him away from the blood and gore. Anything on TV or the computer with death and destruction in it is his automatic favorite." Obviously, the approach we take with these types of kids must reflect their greater needs for limits and supervision. Listed below are additional tips for parents with these types of children:

Additional Tips for Parents of Extremely Challenging Kids
- The child should use the computer only under direct supervision.
- Do not allow the computer to be just another battle in your home.
- Don't ignore what underlies your child's misuse of the computer.

The child should use the computer only under direct adult supervision.
Simply stated, kids with serious emotional or behavioral difficulties SHOULD NOT be allowed unsupervised access to the Internet. This means that a loving and friendly adult MUST be seated next to them every time they use this potentially dangerous tool. Too many disturbed youth surf the Web unsupervised, gravitate toward violent or sexualized content, and become more and more obsessed with the dark side of life. Every time a child like this obtains access to such information, their problems become deeper and more difficult to reverse. Although we can't control whether they use their friend's

computers, or gain access to the Net in some other fashion, we can control what happens in our own homes. How about an example?

Parent:	I want to be with you when you are using the Internet.
Child:	But why?
Parent:	Why do you think?
Child:	I don't know. Why?
Parent:	I like to know what you are looking at.
Child:	You don't trust me.
Parent:	I love you too much to argue.
Child:	Well this sucks!
Parent:	I love you too much to argue.
Child:	You're just using that stupid Love and Logic crap on me!
Parent:	I love you too much to argue.
Child:	Not fair!
Parent:	Would you rather be respectful and have your computer or disrespectful and have me lock it up?
Child:	(Rolling his eyes) OK.

Do not allow the computer to become just another battle in your home.

At this point, the wise reader is probably thinking something like this, "All of this supervision stuff sounds just great until my kid starts arguing constantly about it or starts to get sneaky and tries to use the thing behind my back. What do I do then?"

GET RID OF IT! That's right! An electronic device of any kind is not worth fighting with your kids over! If frequent battles revolve around the television, computer, stereo, or video game, give them to a friend for safekeeping until your kids prove to you that they can be polite, respectful, and get their chores done. See how long it takes them to gain a new appreciation of your word.

WISE WORDS
It's really hard to surf the Net without a surfboard. Wise parents remove the computer as soon as it becomes an object of constant hassles or conflict.

WARNING! THIS WILL ONLY WORK IF YOU CAN DO IT IN A LOVING YET FIRM WAY! Notice how the parent below delivers this consequence without warnings, sarcasm, or anger:

Child: Where is my computer?

Parent: (Very sincerely) This is so sad. I had to lock it up.

Child: What? Are you crazy?

Parent: You may use it again when I'm sure we won't be having arguments about it—and I'm sure you won't be sneaky about using it.

Child: I hate you.

Parent: I know.

Child: You're stupid.

Parent: I'll be happy to listen when your voice sounds calm like mine. I'll be in my room reading.

Don't ignore what underlies your child's misuse of the computer. Kids ask for help in a variety of ways. Rarely do they approach their parents and say, "My self-concept is so poor that I really don't believe I can be successful with friendships. I feel so bad about this that I just find it a lot easier to lock my bedroom door and spend all evening on the computer. I think it's time for me to get some professional help."

Over their bowl of cereal in the morning, even fewer children blurt out, "I really need some professional help because of my obsession with blood, gore, violence, and hate on the Internet."

Kids frequently ask for help by acting-out. Their behavior is the messenger. The message is simply, "I'm feeling so bad inside that I don't know what to do. I'm not getting what I need right now. Please help!"

If you are at all concerned that your child might be asking for help, don't ignore your worries! Discuss them with a therapist who understands children and families, and get their advice on how you can best help your child. WARNING! AVOID THERAPISTS WHO DON'T SPEND TIME UNDERSTANDING AND HELPING BOTH YOUR CHILD AND YOU. The most effective therapists spend time alone with the child, but they also take time to give parents practical ideas and tools. In my (Charles') own experience as a therapist, kids always got better significantly faster when their parents spent time in my office as well.

FOR YOUR THOUGHTS

1. Might it be worth experimenting with an "electronics-free" weekend?
2. If your child gets very irritable or angry when they are not allowed to surf the Net, what might this be telling you? For a hint read page 94.
3. Is it wise to give a lengthy explanation for why you want the computer in the family area instead of your child's room? Read page 96 for a hint.
4. Have you recently had an honest discussion with your child about the pros and cons of the Internet? What tends to happen when we send positive expectations about our children's ability to make wise choices about the negative content?
5. Are you willing to allow an electronic device to interfere with loving relationships in your family?

CHAPTER 13

WISE WORDS

*When a child says, "I hate you," they are really saying,
"I'm doing everything I can to manipulate you and
it isn't working! I want my way!"*

When our sweet angels say, "I hate you," it may sting us at first, but it may be a signal that we are moving in the right direction. Right direction? How is hearing your kid say, "I hate you" moving in the right direction? When kids try to manipulate through arguing, and their parents start using Love and Logic to short-circuit this bad habit, the kids get really mad! This frustration and anger on the child's part signals the parent that healthy control over the home is returning to its rightful owner—the parent!

An example makes this point clearer. Once upon a time there was a small country inhabited by hard working people. These people worked hard but were very angry with their king, who was quite a dictator. One day, they decided to overthrow this powerful king by forming a small army. Their army marched bravely toward the castle. Did the king surrender peacefully? Or did he put up a great fight? A tremendous battle took place as the king tried to defend his throne. The farther the people's army marched, the more soldiers the king sent. The battle intensified, but the hard working people eventually took control of their country. They lived happily ever after.

When kids begin to run the home by arguing and manipulating, they become very much like the king in this story. They get addicted to power and soon become dictators. When parents gather an "army" of Love and Logic techniques, the child will gather his or her own army. His or her defense of the throne will include a wide range of "weapons" ranging from subtle guilt trips, such as "If you loved me..." to intense temper tantrums. "I hate you" represents the child's last ditch attempt to regain the throne. When parents hold firm and resist arguing with this barb, they begin to regain loving control over the home. And there is a much better chance that everyone will "live happily ever after."

WISE WORDS
The only throne a child should sit on is in the bathroom. Kids always feel safer and more loved when Mom and Dad are queen and king in a loving, gentle way.

Hearing "I hate you" still hurts, even when we understand that our kids really don't mean what they are saying. As parents, each and every one of us has a very strong need to feel loved by our children, so these types of words cause us real pain. This need to feel loved is very normal. It only becomes abnormal and unhealthy when we avoid setting firm limits, or let our kids off the hook, in fear of losing their friendship or affection.

WISE WORDS

Wise parents aren't afraid of their kids getting mad at them. They understand that children can hate what their parents do—while still loving their parents very much. Wise parents also teach their kids that it is OK to be mad but not OK to hurt others with words or actions.

How do we teach our kids not to say such hurtful things? A good dose of reality usually does the trick! The most "real" thing about human relationships is that you never get more of anything than you give to another. You never get more love than you give—more control than you give—more respect than you give—etc. People at the universities, such as psychologists, sociologists, and other "ists" sometimes call this "Exchange Theory." Exchange theory states that people tend to "exchange" equal doses of what they receive in relationships. Non-"ist" types simply say, "treat others the way you want them to treat you." The Golden Rule goes a long way in relationships.

The quickest way to teach kids about Exchange Theory and the Golden Rule is not to "exchange" goodies for nasty, disrespectful behavior. That is, when our little sweeties say sour things, we experience a "parental energy drain." Such energy drains keep parents from doing things the child wants, and this teaches the child that treating people poorly has negative consequences. Once created, a parental energy drain can only be cured in one of the following ways. First, the child may do some of the parent's chores in payment for the drain. Secondly, the parent might rest instead of doing some type of strenuous activity, such as taking the child to the amusement park, movies, or ice cream at Dairy Land. Thirdly, the parent might go on a brief vacation to one of these fun places, while the kid stays home and pays for his or her own babysitter.

Caution! Some parents apply this technique in a way that backfires. They unwittingly sabotage themselves because they are led astray by one of two very common parenting myths.

ENERGY DRAIN MYTH #1
Kids won't learn from their mistakes unless they know how mad they make us.

Parents who believe this myth try their hardest to use the "energy drain" technique, but their kids continue to say nasty, hurtful things. Why? Kids don't just manipulate to get their way. This is only half of the puzzle. Children also love the entertainment of a shocked, worried, angry, or frustrated adult. When parents refuse to give in but continue to show plenty of entertaining emotions, the nasty words have still worked for the child. The child sits back, smiles, and seems to think, "Wow! Look at me! I'm just a kid, but boy can I get to my dad. Look! I can change the color of his face, the tone of his voice—I bet I can even control the potential longevity of his cardiovascular system. Look at me!"

WISE WORDS
Anger and frustration feed misbehavior. Wise parents understand that sadness is a much better teacher than anger.

ENERGY DRAIN MYTH #2
Consequences must be delivered immediately.

Another reason parents tend to get caught in the "anger and frustration" trap is due to the very common belief that consequences for misbehavior must be delivered immediately. Don't fall into this trap! How many of us are good at coming up with an immediate and logical consequence when our child is saying hurtful things or has just done something like wrecking the family car? And, how many of us are good at using sadness instead of anger under these circumstances? One parent joked that she actually has a bunch of "great" ideas at times like these—retroactive birth control, paying kidnappers to take her kid, etc.

WISE WORDS
Wise parents wait until they are calm and have a solid plan before delivering consequences.

Let's take a look at how two different parents used Love and Logic to teach kids about the Golden Rule:

Child:	Daaaad. Why can't I have that coat? All my friends have one like that.
Parent:	Feel free to buy it as soon as you've earned enough money.
Child:	But I want you to buy it. Please!
Parent:	Nice try.
Child:	Buy why?
Parent:	What did I say?
Child:	You never get me anything.... I hate you!
Parent:	(Whispering in a sad tone of voice) This is so sad. I'll have to do something about this. Try not to worry.

The next day after the parent has calmed down and developed a plan

Child:	Daaaaad! Will you take me over to Randy's?
Parent:	(With sadness) I'd love to, but I'm so drained from all your arguing yesterday. I just don't have the energy.
Child:	Aw Dad. Come on.
Parent:	I'll probably have enough energy if you mow the lawn for me first so I don't have to do it later.
Child:	But that's slave labor.

Parent: (Smiling) What I like about you most is your sense of humor.
Child: Well, I'll just stay home.
Parent: It will be nice to have you home.

This parent used the energy drain technique by offering to do things for the child only after being "recharged." Recharging takes place only after the parent rests instead of doing something the child wants—or when the kid does one of the parent's chores.

Let's take a look at another way of using the energy drain technique:

Child: I hate you!
Parent: Are you sure saying that is wise? Do you think something sad might happen?
Child: That's stupid! I hate you!
Parent: That is sad.
Child: I don't care what you do.
Parent: (Walking away) I love you too much to fight with you about this.

The next weekend
Child: Where are you going?
Parent: Adventure Land amusement park
Child: This is going to be great!
Parent: (With sincere sadness) This is so sad. You aren't going.
Child: What?
Parent: I started thinking about how you told me that you hated me. And, I got worried that you might say that out in public. That would be a real energy drain for me.
Child: But I won't say it again.
Parent: I know.
Child: Can I go?
Parent: This is sad—no.
Child: Why? That's not fair! You can't leave me here alone!
Parent: Don't worry. You are hiring a babysitter for today.

> She'll be here before we leave. She'll tell you how
> much you need to pay her.
Child: I don't have any money—I can't pay.
Parent: No problem—I'll pay the sitter, and you can pay
         me back with chores.
Child: I'm not doing any chores—that's not fair.
Parent: (Still in a sad tone of voice) That's OK, because
         you can also pay me with some toys. You decide.

This parent applied the energy drain technique by planning a
little "recharging session" for herself, made possible in part by
her child paying for a babysitter. Although some parents might
believe this approach to be a bit extreme, those who use it are
amazed at how quickly their kids learn NOT to say nasty
things like, "I hate you!"

FOR YOUR THOUGHTS

1. Do you know any parents who continue to meet each and
   every one of their child's demands though the child habitually
   says nasty things like "I hate you"?
2. What rule of Love and Logic are such parents violating? See
   pages xxiv-xxv for these two rules.
3. Is it wise to take "I hate you" personal? Or is it smarter to
   say to yourself, "Looks like she's experimenting with a new
   argument. It's my job to prove that it won't work."
4. Might it be smart to find a babysitter long before you actually
   need one? Would you feel more confident knowing that you
   had someone ready and waiting just in case you had a
   severe energy drain?
5. Will a child be harmed for life if he has to pay a babysitter
   with his CD player? Will a child be harmed for life if he
   learns that being nasty and manipulative is the best way to
   get what he wants? Which is going to hurt a child in the
   long run? Which will help the child?

CHAPTER 14

How am I supposed to have any friends when you guys treat me like a baby?

If it would help, you might tell them that your parents still live in the Dark Ages.

WISE WORDS

*Wise parents realize that it is more difficult to
make good decisions when issues center around
their own childhood fears or pains.
Wise parents don't allow OTHER parents' rules to
dictate how they run their own homes.*

It is natural for parents to be concerned and to foster feelings of fear when they are confronted with the possibility that their kid will be considered "different" from others. Most parents remember being rejected by other kids at times. These are usually very painful memories. Feeling different is very hard for most teens—and many adults!

In many cases the pain of these rejection experiences was severe enough that the person's natural defense mechanisms kicked in. One of these mechanisms serves to suppress the memories of painful experiences to the point that they are remembered only under extreme conditions. If our minds didn't have this ability to repress bad experiences, we would all be awash in pain to the point of not being able to lead our lives in a healthy way.

This psychological phenomenon helps us understand how abused children grow up to abuse their own children. One would think that the pain of childhood abuse would cause a child to grow to adulthood with such vivid memories of how bad it feels to be abused that they would never hurt another person. It's natural to think that an adult who was burned by cigarettes as a child could never do that to their own children.

Why is the opposite sometimes true? Childhood abuse is extremely painful because it triggers a child's worse fear—that of being rejected by the parent. This fear is so great that a child's defense mechanism locks in, usually by helping the youngster see different reasons for the adult's abusive behavior. It is far too painful for a child to think, "My parent doesn't love me." It is far easier for his mind to paint a different, and more acceptable, reason for the actions of the parent.

This helps us understand the often-heard phrase, "My dad whipped me with the belt and it didn't hurt me. Look how I turned out. He did it because he loved me." This is the picture the mind of a terrified, helpless little child conjured up to avoid the horrible thoughts of, "Maybe my dad doesn't love me." As the years roll by, this new picture becomes increasingly vivid to the person. This person is one who grows up very likely to "knock some sense" into his own kids—without seeing any wrong in it.

What's the point here? All of us grow up having painful memories of some kind. If we are lucky, they are not centered around abuse or some other extremely sad event or events. The lesson here is that repressed memories of pain play a large role in how we relate to our kids, even though we are often unaware of them. Parents who experienced peer rejection as kids often have a much harder time setting and enforcing limits when their own kids say things like, "Nobody will like me" or "How am I supposed to have any friends when you treat me like a baby?" Isn't it amazing how our kids quickly learn to push the most painful buttons?

The unfortunate result is that parents often have a much harder time doing effective discipline around issues that were especially painful for them as children. For example, some parents experienced so much peer rejection as kids that they allow their own children to do inappropriate things just to keep friendships with the "in" crowd. Do you know any parents who allow their kids to stay out all night? Do you know any who buy their kids anything they want so they won't look un-cool? We know of a high school student whose mother allowed him to drink beer and sleep with his girlfriend in their home—just so he wouldn't have to experience the pain of rejection. How sad! If you listen to these parents, they often have some interesting ways of explaining away their kid's bad behaviors. We've all heard their excuses.

Common Excuses Made by Some Parents
- All kids try drugs.
- All kids drink.
- Kids are all just more sexually active these days.
- I don't want my kid to hate me.
- Friendships are just so important. Kids need to be kids.

WISE WORDS

Wise parents know that kids will use guilt only if it works on their parents. And, wise parents never allow guilt to guide their parenting.

There is an interesting difference between kids and adults. Kids quickly abandon any techniques that don't work. If pouting doesn't help them get their way, they give it up and try other approaches until they find the one that gets the job done. On the other hand, many adults tend to try an approach, discover it doesn't work, and then use it over and over again with increasing amounts of intensity.

Once parents understand that kids will abandon those techniques that don't work, they can be much more confident that learning and using new parenting skills will force their kids to act more responsibly. Therefore parents who don't knuckle under to guilt soon find that their kids stop resorting to its use.

A WORD OF CAUTION
Kids who see their parents getting frustrated by a guilt trip, are given a sense of hope that this manipulation maneuver might work the next time.

WISE WORDS
Wise parents remember:
"Never let your kids see you sweat!"

It is not uncommon for parents to see their children repeatedly using the same techniques to get their way, even when those techniques don't produce the desired results. The reason for this lies in the fact that the parents had to work too hard to convince their youngsters that they were not going to get their way. In other words, the parent displayed anger and frustration while setting the limit.

Ironically, these intense situations are often rewarding to children. Some kids find that they are drawn to angry confrontations because of the excitement and attention these situations provide. Another negative outcome is that the youngster is left with an impression that he/she had almost won. It's almost as if they reason, "Wow! That almost worked. Mom and Dad got really mad! A little more practice with my manipulation skills might just get me what I want." The end result is that the parent and the child become locked into an ongoing cycle of confrontations and arguing.

This helps us understand why it is so valuable to use the Love and Logic One Liners—and why it is so valuable to use them with calmness instead of anger. We often teach parents to use a One Liner that not only neutralizes the argument, but also helps the parent avoid feeling mean or insensitive. This is especially important when parents are dealing with their own childhood memories of pain. Notice how effective this One Liner is in the following situation:

Teen: Roger's dad rented a room at the Biltmore Hotel so we can have an all night party to celebrate Homecoming. Everybody's going to be there. It's going to be so cool. I've got to go.

Parent: Oh, really. An all night party? What goes on at an all night party? Political discussions?

Teen: Oh, Mom. Don't be silly. We all just get together and hang out.

Parent: That takes all night at a hotel?

Notice that the parent is calmly collecting information before jumping into an argument about the wisdom of an all night party in a hotel. Parents can learn a great deal during this stage of the conversation if they remember to listen to the answers without being judgmental. Making judgments will be much more important and effective later in the discussion.

The technique of simply collecting information without arguing can have a powerfully disarming effect. Notice also that the parent does not react one way or the other to each of the teen's answers. The parent just continues to ask innocent questions.

Teen: Yeah, that's what kids do. We just hang out and party, and you know...

Parent:	Does that include drinking, drugs, making out?
Teen:	Well, sure, with some kids. But that happens everywhere. That stuff doesn't happen just because it's in a hotel room, but you know I don't do that kind of stuff.
Parent:	So how does Roger's dad arrange for a bunch of underage kids to have a hotel room all to their own for the whole night? Are there some adult chaperones with the group?
Teen:	Well no. He trusts his kids. It's not like you and Dad. He doesn't treat his kids like babies.

It would be very tempting for the parent in this situation to launch in a lecture about Roger's father's lack of legal responsibility. That might be a good thing to discuss, but not at this moment. It can be done more effectively at a different time. A wise parent does not allow the discussion to go off in different directions. It is important to stay focused on the issue at hand.

Parent:	So, not allowing kids to have an all-nighter in the hotel is treating them like babies?
Teen:	Right. How can I ever have any friends if you and Dad treat me like a baby and I have to tell my friends I can't come just because my parents are still living in the Dark Ages. (Notice there isn't a question mark at the end of this sentence? It wasn't really a question. It was an accusation.)
Parent:	I wouldn't feel like a responsible parent if I let you go to that party. You can do that when you are living on your own.
Teen:	Well, that's stupid. You don't care if I have friends or not.
Parent:	I love you too much to argue about that.
Teen:	You just don't want to see me grow up. I'm not going to stay little forever, you know.
Parent:	I love you too much to argue.
Teen:	I suppose that no matter what I say, you're just going

Parent: to keep saying that. How stupid! Can't you say anything else? What am I supposed to tell my friends, that I can't come because I'm still a little baby?

Parent: If it would help, you might tell them that your parents still live in the Dark Ages and that they're totally unreasonable and you can't even argue with them. If that doesn't work, you might tell them that you can't come because your parents will kill you if you do. I'm sure they'll understand.

Teen: That's stupid.

Parent: You may also try telling them that your parents are so old fashioned that they actually call the police when they know that an underage drinking party is going on.

Teen: You wouldn't.

Parent: I love you too much to allow dangerous, illegal things to go unreported.

FOR YOUR THOUGHTS

1. What might the teen have said if the parent had reacted to the kid's request to attend the party with, "Are you crazy? You're not going to be any part of an all night party at a hotel. I know what goes on at those things, so just forget it!"

2. How might the discussion have progressed if the parent had launched into a lecture about the legalities of what Roger's dad was doing by renting a hotel in his name for a group of underage children?

3. How did the parent give the teen a way to save face with the friends? Refer to the parent's last statements on page 119.

4. How long could the parent continue to fall back on the One Liner, "I love you too much to argue."

5. Why should a parent report this type of party to the police? HINT: Because reporting it would be the morally, ethically, and legally correct thing to do!

CHAPTER 15

WISE WORDS

Wise parents know that good discipline and logical consequences still work, even when their kids roll their eyes and say, "I don't care if you do that."

"So what. Go ahead and discipline me. I don't care." Imagine the feelings these words bring to heart when we hear them from the mouths of babes. Our hearts sink and our blood pressures rise. And, it's not just the words that disturb us! It's the look that so commonly goes along with them. THE LOOK is hard to describe yet packs a powerful punch—shoulders scrunched-up—eyes rolled back in their socket—jaw dropped.

Why is this so upsetting? Well, we want our kids to care about these types of things! When they don't, we begin to worry. The more we worry, the more we begin to entertain a wide variety of uncomfortable thoughts:

- What's wrong with this kid? Why doesn't he care?
- Doesn't care? Doesn't care? What kind of life is she going to have if she doesn't care?
- What have I done to make her not care?
- For cryin' out loud! He doesn't care? I'll MAKE him care!
- Serial killers don't care. What am I going to do?

What's a parent to say or do when their child says, "Discipline me! I don't care."

WISE WORDS

Wise parents never waste words trying to talk their kids into caring.

DO NOT fall into the trap of trying to convince your child to care about a consequence! The more words you use, and the more energy you expend, the more frustrated you will be. In the discount department stores of life, have you ever seen a child's eyes glaze over as their parent eloquently gave the "you-better-care-about-this" lecture? And, have you ever seen the nasty little grin that tends to appear on a child's face as the parent's forehead begins to sprout veins? And, have you ever heard a frustrated parent finally say, "You think this is funny young man? You wipe that smile off your face! I mean it!" I witnessed the following "conversation" between a father and his teenage daughter:

Child: Daaaad! I don't want those kind of pants. They're like soooo five minutes ago.

Parent:	What? Five minutes ago? What are you saying?
Child:	They are like sooo old-fashioned and dorky. I want these instead.
Parent:	No way! Those cost almost fifty dollars.
Child:	This is like sooo stupid.
Parent:	That's it. For crying out loud, we are leaving. You're just going to have to go without new pants if you are going to be that way.
Child:	(Rolling her eyes) Soooo. I don't care.
Parent:	(With bulging veins and a tomato-red face) You better start caring, young lady. How many times do I have to tell you? Life is not some big joke.
Child:	(Begins to grin)
Parent:	Oh! Oh! You think this is a big joke. You just wait. You're in seventh grade right now, but real life is just around the corner. Then you're going to care. It's not some bowl of cherries out there, you know.
Child:	I don't care.

Now for the good news! This type of sad situation doesn't have to happen! And, if it does, there are practical ways to get unstuck. Many kids really DO care about consequences but will do almost anything NOT to admit this to their parents! Listed below are some reasons for this:

Why kids who DO CARE about a consequence refuse to admit it:
1. To save face
2. To regain control
3. To get an entertaining show of parental frustration and anger

Some children desperately want us to believe that they are tough and can handle anything. These kids will do almost anything to make us believe that they don't care. They can be so convincing! They might even smile or laugh as they are saying, "I don't care." When we take a deeper look at these kids, we realize that they really do care. Their bravado or nonchalance is merely a smoke screen.

Many children will also say they don't care as a way of regaining control and obtaining a wonderful show of parental frustration and anger. Through experience, these kids have learned that all it takes is a roll of one eye, a slight grin, and a monotone, "I don't care" to get Mom or Dad to go into the "you-better-care-about-this" lecture. As the lecture continues, they think to themselves, "Look at me! Look how powerful I am. Look what I can do to my parent!"

Kids that say they don't care, but really do, can be loads of fun to work with! YES! With the right reply, we can quickly neutralize the power struggle. Here's an example:

Child: Daaaad! I don't want those kind of pants. They're like soooo five minutes ago.

Parent: What? Five minutes ago? What are you saying?

Child: They are like sooo old-fashioned and dorky. I want these instead.

Parent: The ones you want are thirty-five dollars more. How are you going to pay for the difference.

Child: What? Pay?

Parent: I want you to have the pants you want. I will pay the amount equal to the one's you don't like, and you can pay the extra with your own money. How does that sound?

Child: That's sooo like stupid.

Parent: (In a calm, sad tone) How sad. I guess we are leaving without anything today. What a drag.

Child: I don't care.

Parent: (With great relief) Thank goodness. That makes it a lot easier for both of us.

Child: But I need those new pants.

Parent: (Whispering as they walk) I thought you didn't care. Let's go home.

WISE WORDS

When a child says, "I don't care if you do that," the wise parent enthusiastically responds, "Oh thank goodness! That makes it a lot easier for both of us."

Some children really don't care much about consequences. This can happen for a variety of reasons. One reason is that the child has actually been trained, by his or her parents NOT to care. What? How can this be? Let's take a look at three things that well-meaning parents do that result in this happening.

How to train your child not to care about a consequence:
1. Warn them about the consequence in advance
2. Deliver the consequence with sternness or anger
3. Gradually increase the size of the consequence you use

When parents repeatedly warn about consequences in advance, children quickly learn to brace themselves. In other words, many children tend to talk themselves out of caring about consequences when they've been told about them in advance. In contrast, when consequences are delivered without warnings, there is no time to do this. Below are two examples. One illustrates the effects of warnings—a child who says he doesn't care. The other shows the power of consequences without warnings—a child who does care.

EXAMPLE #1:
Consequences with repeated warnings

Friday
Parent: Didn't I already tell you? If you don't clean that yard, you are not going to the Fair with us on Sunday.
Child: OK. I'll get to it.
Parent: I mean it. If that isn't done, you're not going.
Child: OK. I said I'll do it.

Saturday

Parent: The yard isn't done yet! You know what's going to happen if you don't get it finished, don't you?

Child: I know.

Parent: You aren't coming to the Fair with us tomorrow if it isn't done.

Sunday

Parent: The yard isn't done. This is really sad, but you can't come with us.

Child: (In a nonchalant tone) I don't care. The Fair is stupid anyway.

And the battle continues

EXAMPLE #2:
Consequences without repeated warnings

Friday

Parent: Would you like to have the yard cleaned by tomorrow or have it done Sunday morning so you can come with us to the Fair?

Child: I'll get it done by Sunday morning.

Parent: Super! Thanks for your help.

Saturday

Parent: (Notices that the yard is not done but bites her tongue and says nothing)

Sunday

Parent: (Notices that the yard is not done but still says nothing)

Child: Is it time to leave for the Fair yet?

Parent: This is so sad.

Child: What?

Parent: What did you say you would get done by this morning?

Child: I didn't have a chance.

Parent:	This is really sad. I take kids special places when they are getting their chores done. I'll call Ms. Bartlett from next door. She'll come by to watch you.
Child:	But that's not fair.
Parent:	(With her hand gently on the boy's shoulder) I know. This is such a drag. I hope you can come next time.

Love and Logic parents also know that providing repeated warnings gives kids a distorted view of the world and how it works. In other words, repeatedly warning a child about consequences trains them to believe that someone will follow them throughout their lives warning them to make wise choices.

WISE WORDS
Wise parents know that most real world consequences come without warnings. They parent in a way that creates a voice inside of their children's heads. This voice says, "If I make a bad choice, something bad or even dangerous could happen—without any warnings."

A second way of training children not to care about consequences is to deliver them with sternness or anger. Human nature is strong. And, one very basic aspect of human nature is to blame others for our mistakes. Most adults learn to override this tendency and accept responsibility for their actions. Many children and teens are not quite this mature. When we deliver consequences with sternness or anger, the child is given a perfect opportunity to blame us for their pain. Instead of seeing the consequence as a logical and reasonable outcome of their behavior, they see it as the adult's way of getting even. When this happens, many children will say, "I don't care." What they are really saying is, "I don't care, because it's not my fault. If you weren't so mean, I wouldn't have done this in the first place." In contrast, when consequences are delivered with sincere empathy, kids find it much harder to shift the blame.

WISE WORDS
Kids won't care about consequences if they're distracted by the redness in their parents' faces.

Lastly, children can be trained not to care about typical consequences by slowly being exposed to gradually larger ones. To understand this concept, let us consider a quick experiment. First, put one hand in a cool sink of water and gradually increase the temperature by adding more and more hot water. By gradually increasing the temperature in this way, most people can stand some pretty hot water! Similarly, children can be trained not to care about all but the "hottest" consequences. This happens when parents are afraid to deliver reasonably significant and meaningful consequences when the misbehavior begins. Instead, some parents provide a very small consequence or warning when the misbehavior starts. As the misbehavior continues, they provide a slightly larger one. When this fails, they up the ante just a bit—and so on. Ironically, this strategy usually results in parents having to use heavier consequences in the long run.

On with our experiment. Now, plunge your dry hand directly into the hot water. This hand isn't used to the heat, and most people really feel the difference! Clearly, kids also care more about consequences when they aren't used to the "heat" of many smaller ones.

WISE WORDS
Parents who use larger and more meaningful consequences when misbehaviors just begin, find that they have to use fewer consequences in the long run. They also notice that their kids are happier and better behaved.
Parents who use smaller and less meaningful consequences when misbehaviors begin, find that they have to use many more consequences—and larger ones in the long run. They also notice that their kids are resentful and poorly behaved.

A final reason some kids say they don't care is because they feel too sad or depressed to care. Growing up has never been easy. In today's world, it's harder than ever! Many children in this country live day-to-day with tremendous feelings of sadness. When this sadness lasts long enough, and when it begins to creep into more and more parts of their lives, children begin to say to themselves and others, "I don't care." This type of "don't care" is very real to the child. And, this type of "don't care" is NOT manipulative.

Depression in children is not always easy to spot or diagnose. Why? Every child expresses his or her sadness in a different way. Further, some of the symptoms of depression in children and teens look much different than those seen in adults. Below is a list of some common symptoms seen in depressed kids.

Some symptoms of depression in children and teens
1. Irritability or a "nasty attitude"
2. A change toward more misbehavior
3. Hyperactivity or lethargy
4. Withdrawal from friends and activities (Alone in his or her room for extended periods)
5. A drop in grades
6. Significant appetite changes (Eating much less or much more)
7. Frequent statements like, "I'm stupid" or "I hate myself"
8. Suicidal comments like, "I wish I was never born"
9. Lack of interest in previously enjoyed activities
10. Changes in sleep patterns (Sleeping a lot more or a lot less)

What's a parent to say or do when they see these potential symptoms in their kids?

WISE WORDS
Wise parents don't hesitate to get professional help when their kids show signs of depression.

There is great news for kids and adults with depression! Scientific advances and improvements in therapy have resulted in many very successful treatments! The most important thing parents can do is reach out to a competent mental health professional for help. Parents can do a lot to help their kids, but severe sadness and depression won't go away without professional help.

WISE WORDS
Therapists who only work with the child—without working with the parents as well—usually have much poorer results.

In addition to good therapy, parents and teachers can make a major positive impact on really sad or depressed kids just by noticing positives. Being noticed as competent and important is a basic human emotional need. CAUTION! Do not fall into the trap of trying to convince the child that he or she is good. This won't work! There is a major and important difference between noticing positives and trying to convince someone that they are good. Here are examples of each:

Noticing	Trying to Convince Someone They are Good
I noticed you like to draw.	You are such a great artist. Wow!
I noticed you play a lot of football.	You are such a wonderful athlete.
I noticed other kids really hang around you.	You are so handsome. Everybody likes you.
I noticed you got that problem on your homework right.	You got that right. You are so smart.

Wise parents and teachers take the tack of merely noticing positive things about children without judging. That is, they don't end "I've noticed that..." with "and that's great!" Why is this the case? Kids who are feeling bad about themselves almost always discount praise. Simply stated, they don't believe us. Noticing is a lot easier for them to take, and they are much less likely to discount what we say. By the way, have you ever noticed how good it feels to feel noticed by someone?

FOR YOUR THOUGHTS

1. Does a child need to be visibly upset to be learning from a consequence? Or can learning even take place when a kid says, "I don't care"?
2. Is it possible that most kids care more about consequences when they have a strong relationship with their parents?
3. Have you ever known someone who was so negative with you that you started to care less and less about disappointing them? Do you think some kids "don't care" because they feel like their parents or other adults never notice the positive things they do?
4. Why is it so tempting to give our kids repeated warnings? Might it be that we love them so much that we want them to avoid making mistakes and to be happy? Of course! Isn't it ironic that repeated warnings actually create unhappy kids who make a lot of mistakes?
5. It's smart to consult with a mental health professional if you suspect your child is suffering from depression. Is he or she showing any of the signs listed on pages 129?

CHAPTER 16

WISE WORDS

Children who learn that temper tantrums work become adults who use them often. Wise parents take control of this problem when the child is still small enough to carry.

Have you ever noticed how fast a three-year-old can develop a severe case of muscular paralysis, become totally limp, fall on the floor, and start screaming something like, "Waaaaaa! I want it! Waaaaa! I want it!"? The fun doesn't really begin until our kids decide to take their show on the road! In the toy aisles and check-out lines of life, is there any better way to hold your parents hostage? Onlookers glance over, take stock of the situation, and rejoice, "Thank goodness that's not my kid!"

Every parent from planet Earth has experienced Toddler Temper Tantrums or the "Triple T's." And the problem doesn't always go away after toddlerhood! This section is devoted to helping parents of young children stay sane, stop tantrums, and make the grocery store a fun place to go with their kids.

WISE WORDS

How parents handle toddler temper tantrums determines how their children will deal with authority figures, disappointments, and anger for the rest of their lives.

Young children are scientists. That's right! Their primary job is to look around and ask themselves over and over again, "I wonder what will happen if...?" Little kids learn about the world and about cause-effect relationships by asking this question and by experimenting. Sometimes the experiments are sweet. For example they may ask, "I wonder what will happen if I kiss Mommy?" or "I wonder what will happen if I say 'Please?'" or "I wonder what will happen if I eat my peas?" Other times the experiments are sour. Instead, they ask, "I wonder what will happen if I spit my peas?" or "I wonder what will happen if I pull Mommy's hair?" or "I wonder what will happen if I get on the floor, wiggle around, and throw a big fit?"

WISE WORDS

All kids experiment with both nice and nasty behavior. Wise parents show their kids that sweetness gets you a lot—nastiness gets you nothing.

All parents want to do the right things for their kids. Nobody sets out ahead of time and wonders, "How can I raise a kid that's obnoxious and nasty to be around?" Unfortunately, some very loving and very well-meaning parents respond to temper tantrums in ways that backfire. Simply said, their reactions unintentionally feed the fire by showing their child that experimenting with nasty behavior pays off. Sadly, kids with these parents come to believe that the best way to get what you want in life is by being nasty or manipulative. How does this happen? Listed below are three ways to train children to throw more fits. For your own sake and your child's, DO NOT fall into these "fit-feeding" traps!

The Appeasement Trap
Some children learn to play water-torture. That is, some kids realize that they can wear their parents down to the point of submission through repeated whining, arguing, and tantrums. And, have you ever noticed how some kids seem capable of sensing when their parents' energy levels are at their lowest and striking with misbehavior at that precise moment? Everyone who's raised kids has at least once given in when they probably shouldn't have. Done rarely, this type of appeasement probably won't create much of a problem. In contrast, doing it often creates children who learn to bully others for what they want. I (Charles) witnessed a sad example of this on the steps of my son's school:

Child: You told me I could take a pack of gum to school today.

Parent: No, Kurt, I didn't. I told you "NO!" Gum is against the rules at school.

Child: (Whining) But why? Not fair! I want it! I want it! I WANT IT!

Parent: I told you why already! Stop whining.

Child: (Crying with every ounce of volume he can muster) Don't leave me! Don't leave me!

Parent: Stop crying. Now look at what you have done.

Everybody is looking. Ok. Have the gum, but don't
ask for anymore this week.

Child: (Starting to calm down)

Parent: Now I mean it! Don't ask again!

Was Kurt's experiment with nastiness a success? In the short-
term, it might have been. He got what he wanted. But, is it
possible that he might start believing that people, especially
women, really don't mean it when they say, "No!" Farther
down the road, this experiment will backfire sadly for Kurt.
How successful and happy can a person really be when they
view others with such little respect?

The Therapy Trap

Parents who fall into the Therapy Trap don't appease their kids
by backing down to water-torture and tantrums. Instead, they
unintentionally reward tantrums by trying to do psychotherapy
every time their child throws a fit. In other words, these very
caring and well-intentioned parents heap tons of attention on
their misbehaving children in an attempt to calm them down.
What is the ironic result? Their children are never calm for
long! Instead, they become attention "junkies," relying on
frequent fits to get their "fixes" of parental kudos. True
psychotherapy does not teach people to get their needs met by
being nasty. Instead, it gives them healthy skills for being
honest, forthright, and caring about their feelings. At a potluck
dinner for parents of preschoolers, we got a sad opportunity to
witness a young father falling into the Therapy Trap.

Child: I want to go home! This is boring!

Parent: Sara, be nice. We are staying for a while longer.
         Don't ask again!

Child: I want to go home! I want to go home! I want to
         go home! I want to go home!

Parent: Honey, we are going to stay. Haven't I told you to
         stop that?

Child: (Rolling on the floor, screaming, and bellowing)

••••••••••••••••••••••••

Parent:	(Gets on the floor with the child) Sara, it's OK. Why are you so upset? I'm sorry you feel so bad. We have to stay because Daddy is having a nice visit with his friends. I know it's hard.
Child:	But I hate this place! Hate it! Hate it! Hate it! Hate it! HATE IT!!!
Parent:	(Still on the floor) I know it's hard for you. It can be really boring. Try to hang in there. Do you need a hug? Let me hold you for a while. There is no need to be so upset. I'm just visiting with my friends. (Ironically, this parent is visiting more with the child than the other parents!)

Did you notice how little Sara was able to get more and more attention by becoming more and more out of control? What is she learning about life here? Can we imagine Sara twenty years from now becoming a chronically unhappy and whiny young woman? Isn't it sad when someone believes they have to be unhappy to get their emotional needs met? Caught in a constant bind, people like Sara spend their entire lives going from crisis to crisis, in an attempt to get others' love. Their pursuit is rarely successful and never healthy.

WISE WORDS

The only person who can calm an angry person is the angry person. Wise parents wait until their children are calm to discuss problems.

The Anger Trap
Parents falling into the anger trap also love their kids. They don't want to appease them, so they don't give in to tantrums. They don't want to give them excessive attention during nasty behavior, so they don't try to calm them down. Instead, they unintentionally fall into the trap of fit-feeding by issuing lots of lectures, warnings, or threats. As they become angrier and more frustrated, their child gets more and more attention.

Strange as it seems, many children find this type of parental frustration and anger very entertaining and reinforcing.

WISE WORDS
Wise parents know that anger and frustration feed misbehavior.

The airport is always an interesting place to study family dynamics. Recently I (Charles) viewed a tiny little boy towering over his frustrated father as they were getting ready to board a flight. Let's take a look at how Dad tried to do the right things yet fell intro the trap of feeding the fire.

Child: When is the plane to Grandma's?
Parent: That's the fiftieth time you've asked me, Tony.
               I don't know. The plane's late. I don't know!
Child: But I want to go now!
Parent: Tony! Don't you talk to me like that! That's one!
Child: But I want to go now!
Parent: (His face red as a tomato) I told you to stop that!
               How many times do I have to tell you?! That's two!
               One more time and you are getting a spanking!
Child: (Crying at full force) Waaaaaaaaa! I hate you, Daddy!
Parent: (Veins bulging in his forehead) That's it! Tony,
               you're getting a spanking.

Has little Tony learned to control the tone of his daddy's voice, the color of his daddy's face, and whether daddy has a happy, calm time or an unhappy, chaotic one? How much energy do you suppose his father has at the end of a typical day? Do you worry that little Tony might some day be in charge of choosing his dad's nursing home? Sadly, the future doesn't look too bright for either of them. Let's hope things change before he hits puberty!

Now that we've seen what can make the problem worse, how about some good news? Wouldn't it be great if parents had just a couple very simple tools that were so powerful they actually started looking forward to their kids throwing tantrums? Read on!

The key to ending tantrums, and raising kids who are liked by themselves and others, involves consistently sending the following message through our words and our actions:

Sweetie, the way you get lots of attention in this house is by being nice. We'll have all sorts of fun together! The way you get very little attention in this house is by being nasty. How sad that will be.

Come on! Get real! How's a parent really supposed to send this message when their kids are grating on their last nerve? Wise parents don't give in. Wise parents don't try to soothe the child with words. Wise parents don't yell and spank. Instead, smart parents sing the "Uh Oh Song." What? The "Uh Oh Song?" Sing? Perhaps an example is in order here!

Child: Yucky food. No!

Parent: (In a soft tone of voice) Julie, you can stay at the table with us as long as you act nice.

Child: No nice! No nice! WAAAAAAAAAAAA!

Parent: (Singing in a sweet tone of voice) Uh oh. This is so sad. Looks like a little bedroom time until you can act sweet.

Child: No! Noooooo! (Refuses to walk to her room)

Without saying a word, Mom picks her up, takes her to her room, and gently places her on the bed.

Parent: (In a calm but firm tone) Honey, you can come out just as soon as you can act nice. Do you need the door open or shut?

Child: (Tries to run out of the room) Noooooo!

Parent: (Singing once again) Uh oh. You are not acting nice yet. Back in your room.

Mom gently puts Julie back in her room, walks out, and closes the door behind her. She's even put a latch on the out-

side so she doesn't have to worry about fighting to keep the door shut. Mom sits right outside until Julie is calm. Then she waits about two extra minutes.

Child: (Calm now but very tired out by her fit.)
Parent: (Walking into the room and resisting the urge to yell or lecture) That was so sad. Give me a hug.

Did Mom handle little Julie without breaking a sweat? Do you suppose this child has learned something valuable from the experience? What? When parents use the "Uh Oh Song," their children quickly develop the following ideas about their parents and themselves.

1. My parents can handle me without getting angry or being mean. They must be really strong, and they must really love me.
2. Since my parents are so strong and love me so much, I'm really safe.
3. When I'm being sweet, I get to be around the people I really love. Being sweet brings sweet rewards.
4. When I'm nasty I have to be by myself. Being nasty brings sour consequences.
5. If my parents can handle me without even breaking a sweat, I must be a pretty neat kid!

The great thing about the "Uh Oh Song" is that it doesn't have to be used very often. Now, that's the true hallmark of a powerful parenting technique! Parents who've experimented with it for a week or two find that their children start to do very interesting and very wonderful things without having to be carried or locked in their rooms! Remember little Julie? Let's take a look at what started happening after only two three good "Uh Oh Trips" to her room.

Parent: Julie, I'll be happy to get you some juice as soon as I'm off the phone.
Child: But I want it now!

Parent: (Singing) Uh oh!
Child: I act nice. I act nice.
Parent: (Smiling) Thanks honey.

Why did Julie stop right in her tracks when she heard Mom sing, "Uh oh." This technique gains its power from basic conditioning principles. In other words, "Uh oh" becomes a trigger phrase or cue that says to the child, "If I keep doing this, things are going to be so sad for me. Better stop while I'm ahead."

Over the past few years parent after parent has raved about how helpful this technique is. They seem amazed by how fast it works, how little they have to use it, and how much happier their kids have become. Isn't it fascinating how children are actually happier when parents set loving limits, even if those limits make them very angry in the short-term?

WISE WORDS
Wise parents understand that we must often make our kids mad in the short-term so that they can be happier in the long-term.

Despite its effectiveness, some have argued that locking a child in their room is abusive. These concerns are important to consider and discuss! Let's take a look at the difference between the "Uh Oh Song" technique and child abuse. Child abuse has two basic characteristics. First, the child is being harmed physically or emotionally. Secondly, the child has no control over the situation.

To prevent emotional or physical harm, it's wise to do some planning BEFORE using this technique. Parents can use the following checklist to make sure they can use this technique in a loving and safe way.

Planning Checklist for the "Uh Oh Song"
1. Can I use the technique without anger, lectures, or threats?
2. Can I carry my child without hurting him or her?
3. Have I made sure the room has nothing in it that might be dangerous if my child is having a fit?
4. Am I sure my child won't crawl out of the window?
5. Can I remember to give my child a choice about whether the door is open, shut, or locked?
6. Do I have some safe way of fastening the door shut if my child tries to leave before he or she is calm?
7. Am I willing and able to sit just outside of my child's room and unlock the door as soon as he or she is calm.
8. Can I walk into the room afterwards, give my child a hug, and say, "I love you."

If you answer "no" to any one of these questions, don't use the "Uh Oh Song" until you're ready. Take some time, plan your approach, and say to yourself, "It's OK if I take some time to plan this. My child's worth it!"

Another very important reason why this technique DOES NOT qualify as child abuse has to do with control and who has it. With true child abuse, an adult does something, and the child has no say whatsoever. In other words, with true child abuse, the child cannot do anything to change the situation. With the "Uh Oh Song," in contrast, the child actually has control over a number of very important things. For instance, who decides whether the child goes to the room in the first place? The child through their behavior! If the child behaves, they don't go. Secondly, who decides whether the door is open, shut, or locked? The child! If he or she can stay without trying to come out before the fit is over, the door is left open. Lastly, who decides how long the child stays in the room? The child! How long the child must stay depends on the child's choice of how long they want to throw their fit. The parent is always just outside of the room, ready to open the door when the child is calm and ready to come out.

At this point in our discussion, the really smart reader is

probably thinking something like, "Oh yeah. That's all good and fine, but what do I do when I'm out in public and my child starts to have a melt down?" What's a parent to do when their toddler becomes a toy-aisle-terrorist, and carrying them to their room would require a five-mile hike down the highway or through crowded city streets? Wouldn't it be great if there was a practical and powerful solution to problems like this? Ready for the good news? There is!

The first step is getting the "Uh Oh Song" locked-in at home. Why? What we call a "transfer effect" seems to take place when parents successfully use the technique at home, and their kids hear them sing "Uh oh" in public. It's almost as if the child says to him or herself, "My parents can handle me so easy at home with that song. Maybe they can do the very same thing in the store." Shortly after we started teaching this technique in our classes, a mother wrote us a note that went something like this:

Dear Dr. Fay,

You're "Uh Oh Song" has really helped me with my three-year-old Justin. The other day we were in the store. He was sitting in the cart and started screaming for a toy he wanted. I looked down at him, smiled, and sang, "Uh oh!" He stopped screaming, his eyes got real big, and he asked, "Where do I have to go?" I was shocked! He got so quiet that I actually got to shop in peace!

Thanks for the help!

Sincerely,

A happy shopper

The good and the challenging thing about young kids is how fast they learn. Although this transfer effect helps quite a bit, some kids will begin to reason, "Wait a minute. Why am I so concerned about this 'Uh oh' thing? There's no bedroom in this store! Mom can't do anything to me in here! Let the fun begin!"

· ·

WISE WORDS
Wise parents show their kids that nowhere is safe from the "Uh Oh Song."

Nowhere safe from the "Uh Oh Song"? What does this mean? How about another example?

Child:	I want to leave! I hate it here!
Parent:	We will be going soon. I'm not done shopping.
Child:	(Crawls up on a display rack and starts screaming) I wanna go home! I wanna go home! I wanna go home!
Parent:	Uh oh. Looks like a little corner time. See that corner over there? Let's go. (Parent carries child to a corner near where she is shopping.) Feel free to come out and join me as soon as you stop screaming. (Mom turns around, walks to her cart, and keeps an eye on the kid as she continues to shop.)
Child:	(Begins crawling toward her mother)
Parent:	(Walks over to the child, places her back in the corner, sits down with her, and holds her gently in her lap) Sweetie. I will let you go when you stop screaming.
Child:	Continues to scream and try to get away.
Parent:	(Parent keeps her own mouth shut and gently holds the child in place until the fit is over.)

What is the hardest part about using the "Uh Oh Song" in public? Could it possibly be the embarrassment of sitting with a screaming child in your lap in the middle of the supermarket? I (Charles) vividly remember sitting with my own son on a sidewalk in Boulder, Colorado as he threw one of the most fantastic fits I've ever seen. He wanted popcorn. I said "No." He started to throw a fit. I sang "Uh oh" and carried him to a bench, sat him down, and said, "Sweetie. Feel free to come over by me when you can act nice." Then I walked a few steps away and pretended not to be watching him. Through the corner of my eye, I saw him crawling down the sidewalk in my direction, still screaming, "I want it! Popcorn! Popcorn!" I'll never forget how embarrassed I felt getting down on the concrete, holding him in my lap, and waiting for him to stop yelling! I'll also never forget how comforting it was to keep repeating these words to myself:

I didn't come here to build a lasting relationship with these strangers. My child is way more important than anything any one of these people may think! I didn't come here to impress these people. My child is more important than what they think. My child is more important. My child is more important.

I look back on times like these and giggle. I also look at my son and remark, "What a fun kid! I'm lucky to have a kid who is so nice to be around." Maybe it wasn't entirely luck. Maybe it had something to do with me being willing to suffer some embarrassment in order to do what was best in the long run. Parents who use this technique in public tell us that their kids very quickly learn to stay in the corner or over by a wall—without being held! The key is remaining consistent, not talking with our child as we are holding them, and staying cool instead of showing frustration.

Would you like one more tantrum-tamer for the road? Sometimes the quickest and most fun way of dealing with a tantrum is to act crazier than the kid. That's right! Sometimes the best way of handling even the most fantastic fit is by either encouraging the kid to continue or by doing something else entirely unexpected. One parent I know actually looks forward to her kids throwing fits. When one of them starts screaming for candy in the store, she smiles at him and says, "Nice job sweetie, but I'm a little disappointed. I've seen better fits than that! Let me show you." Jumping up and down, she continues, "See, you should stomp up and down, make your bottom lip get real big, and keep whining, 'I want it, I want it, I want it!'" She says that, before long, she's got the attention of other shoppers, and her kids are practically begging HER to behave. Isn't it fun to turn the tables from time to time?

FOR YOUR THOUGHTS

1 Do you know any adults who still believe that temper tantrums are the best way of getting what they want? Are they much fun to be around?
2. When parents are able to handle their young children's temper tantrums well, is it likely that their teenage years will also go a lot smoother?
3. Some people believe that parents should spend a lot of time and energy trying to soothe their children when they are having fits. As a result, do some kids get more attention when they are acting out than when they are behaving?
4. Who is the only person who can calm an angry child?
5. The "Uh Oh Song" is one of the most powerful ways of helping very young children learn to behave. What does a parent need to do BEFORE experimenting with this technique? See page 142 for a planning checklist.

......♥......

CHAPTER 17

WISE WORDS

When drugs and alcohol are concerned, what a parent doesn't know CAN kill their kids.

Parenting can be a pretty scary job! And nothing is scarier than the thought of your own child—the love of your life—smoking pot, popping pills, or putting a needle into his arm. When we mix in driving and sex, the visions get even more frightening!

There is good news! Most kids somehow manage to get

through their teenage years intact and relatively healthy. For those who do have problems, parents can take some steps to help them successfully navigate the crisis. The first step is doing your very best to know what is going on with your kids. Stated simply, good supervision is essential!

A COMMON PARENTING MYTH
Parents should never search their children's rooms.

Parents have a responsibility to know what is coming in and out of their homes. Two types of very well-meaning parents seem to have kids with the most drug problems. The first category of parent is the one who doesn't check up on their kids out of fear—fear that the child might say, "You don't trust me!" DON'T FALL INTO THIS TRAP! Some of these parents also seem to be afraid of what they might find in their kid's rooms. As a result, they shy away from being in touch with what is really going on.

On a deeper emotional level, kids of these parents seem to say to themselves, "I guess my parents don't really care enough to be involved in my life. I guess it doesn't really matter what I do."

The second type of parent is the one who loves their kids but forces them to rebel by trying to control almost every aspect of their lives. These are the parents who constantly bark orders about what their child wears, what he eats, with whom she makes friends, how she wears her hair, what grades he gets, etc. As a result, their children generally feel frustrated and resentful. Parents of this type often have trouble supervising because their kids have become masters at avoiding them and doing things behind their back. Their children seem to reason, "My parents think they can control me? They can't watch me all the time. I'll show them!"

How does a parent avoid being too uninvolved and at the same time avoid being too controlling? Let's take a look at how a parent might manage this balancing act:

Child: If you trusted me, you wouldn't snoop around in my room so much. It's my room.

Parent: You don't like me looking around in your room.

Child: It makes me feel like a little kid. I hate it!

Parent: It really makes you mad.

Child: Yeah. Why don't you trust me.

Parent: I get scared.

Child: What are you talking about?

Parent: I get scared because I love you so much, and I want to make sure you are OK.

Child: (Irritated) I am OK!

Parent: Some kids get caught up in drugs or other problems, and they really have a hard time asking their parents for help—even when they really need and want it.

Child: I'm not on drugs.

Parent: How do you feel about talking to me if you ever need some help?

Child: I guess it would be OK.

Parent: I just want to make sure you know that I love you and I won't yell or scream at you if you ever need some help.

Child: (Rolling eyes) OK, mom. Will you stop snooping around in my room?

Parent: Sweetheart, I just feel like a better parent if I know what is in your room.

Child: That's dumb.

Parent: I just love you so much.

Child: Why don't you trust me?

Parent: I just love you so much.

Child: This is so stupid.

Parent: I just love you so much.

Child: Well, Susan's parents trust her.

Parent: (Walking away) I'm sorry it makes you feel bad. That's just the kind of parent I am—I just love you so much.

This parent did a number of very powerful and healthy things:
1. She communicated love for her daughter while remaining firm.
2. She focused on feelings rather than arguing.
3. She told her daughter that she was there to help—not to yell, lecture, or punish.
4. She became a broken record by repeating, "I just love you so much."

What's a parent say and do when things don't turn out so rosy? What's a parent say and do when the worst really happens—when they find out their child or teen is using drugs or alcohol?

WISE WORDS
*Denial is more lethal than a gunshot
wound to the head!*

Believing that our child has a drug problem—or is experimenting with drugs and alcohol is one of the most painful things a parent can experience. In our pain, it is often easy to deny what we see or to believe that the problem will "just go away." DON'T FALL INTO THIS TRAP! Although ignoring or denying these types of problems may seem easier in the short run, ignoring or denying may lead to a very sad ending—a life of drug addiction, shattered relationships, employment problems, legal difficulties, depression, and sickness. It may even mean having to attend your own child's funeral. There is great hope for kids who use drugs if we take the problem seriously and get help from a competent mental health professional.

A COMMON MYTH ABOUT KIDS AND DRUGS
All kids try drugs. It's just a phase.

THIS IS NOT TRUE! Most kids do not use drugs! And don't believe for a minute that your child will just grow out of doing drugs! Some kids experiment with drugs for a short period and quit without doing much damage to themselves or others. Other kids experiment with drugs and end up losing their lives. Is this a gamble you're willing to take?

Believing that your child will just grow out of using drugs is dangerous. Just as damaging is making excuses for your child's problem. Excuses shift responsibility for solving the problem away from the person who has it, and they distract us from dealing with the real issue—our child's drug use. Making excuses is all part of the monster called denial. Here are some typical ones we've heard:

It all started when he made friends with Alex. I knew that kid was bad news.

What's the big deal? I smoked a little pot when I was a kid, and I turned out OK.

At least he's just drinking and not doing drugs. (Alcohol is a dangerous drug!)

If we can get her out of this neighborhood, she'll be fine. Maybe some time at Grandma's will do her some good.

He's just been under a lot of stress lately.

The greatest danger of making excuses is that underlying causes of the problem are ignored.

WISE WORDS

Drug use is a symptom of deeper problems that must be addressed with the help of a qualified professional.

No kid was ever cured of doing drugs by being yelled at, lectured, or punished. Punishment and threats don't work, because the problems that contribute to drug use lie on a deeper level. Some of these problems include low self-esteem, depression and anxiety, poor social skills, problems with authority and responsibility, family conflict, and inherited biological factors that increase one's susceptibility. Instead of lectures, threats, and punishment, these kids really need three basic things:

1. Parents who DO NOT rescue them from the logical and natural consequences of their drug use. These consequences include sitting in jail, going to court and having to raise money for their own lawyer, being expelled from school, paying for doctor's bills stemming from medical problems caused by the drug use, etc. These kids desperately need to see that their actions can have painful consequences.
2. Parents who deliver strong doses of love and sadness when these consequences are experienced. This parental love and sadness forces the child to "own" the pain of his or her poor decision, rather than blaming it on the parent's anger.
3. Parents who step in and insist on professional help. This also means a family that is willing to do honest work with this mental health professional.

When parents find drugs (including alcohol), there are four steps they can take to help themselves and their children:

What to do when you suspect (or know) that your child is using drugs.

STEP 1.
Buy yourself some time by using a delayed or "anticipatory" consequence.
Instead of trying to solve the problem immediately and running the risk of saying or doing something you'll be sorry for later, try saying this to your child, "I am so upset and mad right now, I just can't think! That's why I'm not going to do anything about this until I've talked to all of my friends and the police. I'll talk to you about it later."

Sometimes we call this technique the "anticipatory consequence," because it allows two very important things to happen. First, it enables you to take some time, get calm, get some help from others, and "anticipate" how your kid is going to react when he or she hears about the consequences of their actions. Secondly, it allows your child or teen to "anticipate" or consider a wide array of possible consequences. Most kids have told me that they would rather receive an immediate consequence than have to wait and think about what might happen.

STEP 2.
Call the police.
First, wise parents don't break the law by covering up for their kids. Secondly, they also know that having an encounter with the police and the legal system is one of the best things for a kid who might be having these types of problems. When children and teens experience real world consequences for drug use, they are generally more motivated to change. Further, police and sheriff's departments can often assist parents in finding local therapists, programs, and other resources helpful for kids who are having problems.

STEP 3.
Talk to your friends and talk to a professional.
Dealing with problems like these can make a parent feel completely crazy. Most parents experience a wide variety of feelings including fear, anger, guilt, helplessness, worry, sadness, etc. Without the caring ear of a caring friend, these times can be unbearable. Talking with a trusted friend can also give you an opportunity to begin putting together some plans for intervening with your child. Other parents can be valuable sources of support and practical ideas.

Wise parents don't try to solve these problems without first consulting with a qualified professional. A good therapist can literally be the difference between life and death for your child. Consulting with a therapist before talking to your child about your plan can be a huge help. The therapist can help you fine-tune your plan and can help you carry it out with a lot more confidence. The therapist will also be available to help you and your family deal with your child's reaction and to help you and your child work through underlying issues contributing to the problem.

STEP 4.
Tell your child about the plan.
This is the hardest part for many parents. For most of us, it is extremely difficult to remain loving and firm without either giving in or getting angry and yelling. This is why it is so important to first use the delayed or "anticipatory" consequence to get calmed down and to get your thoughts together. Some parents even find it helpful to rehearse what they are going to say before talking to their child. Again, a good therapist can be a big help in preparing a parent for this conversation.

Prepare yourself for a strong, negative reaction from your child. This is normal! In fact, if your child gets mad at you, it probably means that you are moving in the right direction. Just keep telling yourself over and over, "I'm doing the right thing! I'm doing the right thing! I'm doing the right thing!"

Here's an example of how a parent we knew followed these four important steps:

Step 1: Use a delayed or "anticipatory" consequence.
Parent: (After finding drugs in the kid's car) I am so scared and angry right now that I just don't know what to say. I'm going to have to do something about this—but not now. I need to talk with the police and think this over first.
Child: Dad! Why are you calling the police? That stuff isn't mine! I don't know how it got in the car. Somebody must have put it in there. Come on!
Parent: I love you too much to argue with you about this. Having drugs in your car is against the law.
Child: If you loved me, you wouldn't call the police. What am I supposed to do?
Parent: (Walking away) I don't know. I'm sorry you don't think I love you.

Steps 2 and 3: Call the police and talk to a friend.
Dad spent the next day talking to the police, a trusted friend, and a therapist recommended by his family doctor. He also spent plenty of time rehearsing over and over again in his mind how he would talk to his son and how he would keep himself calm.

Step 4: Tell your child about the plan.

Parent: I've decided on a plan to help you with the drugs.

Child: You didn't call the police—did you?

Parent: (In a sad tone of voice) Yes. They just pulled up outside. I also gave them the drugs I found. They are testing them at the lab right now.

Child: You call that help? If you really wanted to help me, you wouldn't have called the police! What am I supposed to do now? I can't believe you did that! I hate you!

Parent: I can understand how you might feel that way. I love you.

Child: What am I going to do? What am I supposed to tell them?

Parent: I don't know. Would you like some ideas?

Child: This is so stupid! What am I supposed to do?

Parent: I'm not sure. Would you like some ideas?

Child: What?

Parent: Some people find out that it's better for them in the long run if they just tell the truth. That way, they can get some help from the people who love them.

Child: Am I gonna have to go to court?

Parent: I think so.

Child: Will you get me a lawyer?

Parent: I'll help you find one. Then, we can talk about how you are going to pay me back for his fees and the court costs.

Child: How am I supposed to do that?

Parent: I'm not sure, but you could always use your car as a form of payment.

Child: I can't believe this!
Parent: I know you really worked hard to pay for that car.
Child: (Silent)
Parent: I also talked with a counselor. I think he can be a big help to all of us. We have an appointment for tomorrow.
Child: This is so stupid.
Parent: (With sincere empathy) This is really hard.

Doing the right thing when your kids are involved with drugs and alcohol is extremely difficult. In the short run, it's so much easier just to pretend there isn't a problem. Give your kids a gift. Show them how to do the "right thing" even when the "right thing" is very hard.

FOR YOUR THOUGHTS

1. Why is it so easy to fall into denial when a child is having serious problems? Is it possible that, down deep, no parent wants to believe that their kids might have such problems? How dangerous is this denial?
2. Is it the end of the world if your child is using drugs? Or are there ways to get help and really up the odds for a happy ending?
3. Do all kids try drugs? Or is this just a very common myth? See page 150 for the answer.
4. How accurate is the following statement: "If we can just keep her away from the drugs, she will be OK."
5. Is drug use often a symptom of other problems, such as low self-esteem, depression, anxiety, family conflict, etc?

CHAPTER 18

WISE WORDS

Wise parents know that it is good for kids to go "first class" as a result of their OWN efforts.

"Mom, you just don't understand. I can't be seen in the wrong kind of clothes. It doesn't matter that they look the same. They just aren't the same. All the other kids will know. Everybody who is 'in' wears the clothes with the right labels. It shows that they belong. Nobody will have anything to do with me. How can I show my face? I might as well be dead! If you cared about me at all, you wouldn't even think of buying me the wrong clothes!"

How many parents do you know who would wilt under this barrage? This kid's salvo makes it difficult for the best of parents to think straight. It's this kind of talk that triggers all of the feelings of rejection that many of us felt from time to time as we went through those tough teenage years. It is very possible that decisions made at this time will be emotionally based decisions—that have more to do with the parent's own fears than what is good for the child.

WISE WORDS
While in the heat of emotion, it's a very poor time to make any kind of decision.

It is totally natural for parents to share the fears, disappointments, and hurts that kids have. As a result, our natural tendency is to try and shield them from the upsets we had as children. When we are in the heat of emotion, this protection instinct is at its height. And, we are much less likely to do what our kids really need us to do in the long run. What is this? Kids need us to set firm limits on what we buy for them, giving them the opportunity to learn that having nice things requires effort, continued struggle, and appropriate sacrifices. In other words, what they need in the long run is to learn that there is no such thing as a free meal and that clothes DO NOT make the man!

Clothes vs. Character?
Let's suppose that your youngster could belong to an elite group of kids who only accept others who wear the right clothes. Would you have some doubts about the character of those friends? Would you be proud to know that your kid was a snob?

I'm sure you don't want your kids to spend much time around other kids who believe that they are entitled to the best simply because of their birth or because of the economic position their parents have earned. Given a choice, I'd much rather my kid hung out with others who were learning to earn and appreciate what they get.

Many kids in our affluent society come to believe that they should have what they want as soon as they want it. This belief is hammered in through advertising targeted at kids, as well as children seeing their peers receive expensive goodies without having to earn them. As a result, many young people develop a twisted view of what they deserve, "I'm entitled to it. Everybody else has it. I should have it. And if I don't have it, it's because my parents are being selfish."

When parents bow to this kind of pressure they make a powerful statement to their offspring, "Looking good, feeling good, and having what you want when you want it, is more important than character." Many parents don't realize that giving in to their kids sends this message. Why? Because buying our kids what they want is often an emotionally based decision about not wanting to upset them. When parents give in, the child's potential upset is diffused, and the parent often feels temporarily relieved. Of course, this only lasts until the next time the kid wants something new. As this cycle continues, the child believes stronger and stronger that having what they want is their birthright. Sadly, the development of character and responsibility takes a back seat to immediate gratification.

I have often heard parents defend these actions by saying, "But doesn't my child have a right to the best I can afford?" The answer to that is ABSOLUTELY NOT! Kids have a right to be loved by their parents, treated with respect, have a roof over their heads, have food in their stomachs and an opportunity to earn an education. Our Bill of Rights gives us the right to life, liberty and the pursuit of happiness. It does not guarantee happiness, designer clothes, or a new convertible to drive to school.

WISE WORDS

Smart parents know how to set limits by agreeing with their kids: "I agree! Those sneakers are great. I'll pay $29.95 toward them. Won't it be great when you've earned enough money to cover the rest?"

Any parent who tries to argue with a youngster about whether or not he/she should have designer clothes is in grave danger of having all of their arguments trashed by the child. Kids play by a different set of rules than adults. While the adult is trying to be reasonable, honest and accurate, the rule for the kid is to win at any cost.

The most powerful position a parent can take is that of agreeing with the child about his/her wants. Of course, this does not mean that the adult will be the one who provides the money to pay for these "wants." This kind of parent believes in the concept of "matching funds." What does this mean? Simply put, a parent might be willing to pay for half of the item as long as the child can earn the remainder. There are some clear benefits to this approach. First, it provides the child with some motivation to struggle and work hard. Secondly, it teaches that extra nice things require extra nice effort. Thirdly, it allows the parent to remain the "good guy."

Kid: Mom, I just can't be seen wearing an outfit that is not designer.

Mom: You'd rather have a designer one?

Kid: It's not that I'd rather. I have to. All the cool kids have them.

Mom: Well, then that's what you ought to have. I agree.

Kid: Oh, thanks, Mom. You're the greatest. Can we go get it today?

Mom: How much is it going to cost?

Kid: Well, it's only $100.00. It's on sale.

Mom: How much do the regular ones without the designer label cost?

Kid: Well they cost $30.00, but I couldn't be seen dead in one of them. Nobody wears them, except maybe kids with no fashion sense. I guess if you don't know anything about clothes you might wear something like that.

Mom: Well, I love you and I'd like you to have what you want. I'll donate $30.00, and if you have the rest of the money, you're in that outfit.

Kid: But Mom. I don't have the rest of the money.

Mom: That's OK. As soon as you do I want to see you wearing that outfit

Kid: But I need it now. You don't want me to look like a hick do you?

Mom: I agree. I want you in that outfit as soon as possible, so the $30.00 is yours as soon as you need it.

Kid: But that's not fair. You're just being selfish.

Mom: I want you to have the best and I'm still willing to contribute $30.00.

Kid: How could you do this? You know I need those now. What am I supposed to do, tell my friends that my parents are cheapskates?

Mom: That might be one solution. Let me know when you want that $30.00.

Kid: But how am I supposed to get $70.00? You want me to study and get good grades. How am I supposed to earn money and get good grades at the same time?

Mom: I don't know. Let me know when you're ready for the $30.00. Right now the offer stands at $30.00. It will be going down at a rate of five dollars for every additional minute I have to deal with this.

Now is a good time for Mom to walk away. This teen is going to be angry over the limit being set, and reasoning will just make the problem worse. Remember, kids seldom get angry when they are getting their way. They only seem to get upset when parents love them enough to set limits.

The technique of matching funds works well. The parent can always adjust the parental contribution to match each unique situation. For example a parent might offer a small contribution for one thing and a larger contribution for something else. The parent has earned the money. The parent gets to decide how to spend it.

WISE WORDS

When parents set limits for kids, kids get mad. When parents don't set limits for kids, kids get mad.
Getting mad at limits is usually an immediate and short-lived situation.
In contrast, the anger and hurt kids experience when parents fail to set limits is delayed yet life-long!

FOR YOUR THOUGHTS

1. When was the last time you passed up an opportunity to help your child learn about how the real world works because you didn't want him/her to be upset or disappointed?
2. Instead of being disappointed in yourself for not doing what was right at the time, think of this experience as a good learning opportunity for yourself. Maybe this situation, in combination with what you are learning from this book, could serve as a great reminder of the kind of parent you are hoping to become.
3. Why is it important never to pick a battle over whether a child "needs" a certain type of clothes?
4. Is it more productive to say something like the following? "Yes! I can understand a teenager wanting a cool shirt like that. I'll be happy to pay for half. How might you earn the money for the rest?"
5. When you say something like the above, will your child get really mad? Or will he or she say something like the following? "Mom. You are right. I am so glad you are setting limits with me on this issue. I just know I'll be happier in the long run."

CHAPTER 19

WISE WORDS

Wise parents know that the best way to get their kids to hate each other is to make them shake hands and say, "I'm sorry."

How many times do parents hear one of their kids screaming something like this, "Daaaad! Brian won't stop picking on me! Make him to stop!"

Then Brian begins to whine, "No I didn't! Lisa started it! Why do I always get blamed for everything around here?"

And Lisa retorts, "'Cause you start everything! That's why.

You little jerkhead!"

Brian continues, "Well, at least I don't act like a spoiled brat all of the time!"

Lisa rolls her eyes, takes a deep breath, and goes for the last word, "You moron! How immature."

Does this sound familiar? Do you ever feel like your kids act more like hungry alley cats fighting over the last mouse in town—than the loving sibs you'd hoped they'd grow to be? And, do you ever feel like your head is about to split open from all of the noise and commotion? YOU ARE NOT ALONE!

What's a parent to say or do when their kids are at each other's throats and the living room looks and sounds like finals at the international wresting championship? There is good news! The first step toward relief is seeing sibling conflicts in a new light. Although our children—our own flesh and blood—sometimes seem to be after flesh and blood, they are actually doing something that can prepare them for a happier life! How is this?

WISE WORDS

Sibling spats are excellent learning opportunities for children. How better to practice the skills necessary for getting along with a tough teacher, a demanding boss, or your future spouse?

The vast majority of sibling conflicts are a typical and normal part of family life. It is normal for siblings to argue, fight, and even give each other a few bruises along the road to adulthood. And, by negotiating childhood conflicts with their brothers or sisters, our kids learn valuable skills for getting along with others. For this learning to unfold, the following must take place in the home:

1. Children must witness their parents working out disagreements in a healthy, nonviolent manner. Kids learn their first

and most powerful lessons about cooperation from watching the adults in their lives solve problems peacefully.
2. Parents must place primary responsibility for solving sibling conflicts on the parties involved—the kids!
3. Parents must be able to say something like, "Hey guys. This fighting is hassling my ears. Please take it someplace else—or pay me to listen to it. You decide."

WISE WORDS
Wise parents realize that yelling, "Stop fighting!" is about as effective as fighting fires with a squirt gun.

Here's an example of how a mom might deal with brother-sister squabbling in the car:

Brother: Mom! Jeannie keeps pushing her elbow into me! Make her stop it.
Sister: Goll! He won't stop making faces at me!
Brother: (Pushing sister) But she's over the line!
Sister: Yeah, but you got to sit by that window last time!
Mom: (With a smile and sadness in her voice) Uh oh guys. Is this going to be an energy drain?
Sister: (Talking to brother) Be quiet! Stop it! Last time Mom had an energy drain in the car we had to pay her back with toys and she wouldn't take us the places we wanted to go. Be quiet!
Brother: (Mumbling while slumping down in his seat) This is dumb.
Sister: (Silent)
Mom: Good thinking guys. Thanks!

Unfortunately, sibling conflicts often become more chronic and serious when one or all of the following take place:

1. The parents get visibly upset about their kids' fighting, start lecturing, and try to make their children get along.

2. The children are not required to repay their parents for any hassles created by the arguing or fighting.
3. Someone consistently compares one sibling with another.

In some families, children learn early on that bickering and fighting gains their parents' attention and enables them to control their parents' emotions. Do kids get together at the beginning of the day and say to each other, "Hey, lets get in a big fight today so Mom and Dad have to pay attention to us and can't have a life of their own." Of course not! Nevertheless, when parents yell or lecture in order to determine "who started it," to get their kids to "knock it off" or to get their children to "say sorry and shake hands," the parents are doing more thinking and worrying than the kids! Soon the children learn on an unconscious level that they can control the color of their parents' faces, the volume of their voices, their reserves of emotional energy, and the potential longevity of their cardio-vascular systems. And, have you ever noticed how your kids tend to start a fight just as you start talking on the phone or start a quiet conversation with your spouse? What better way to control your parents!

WISE WORDS
There is no case of sibling rivalry that can't be made worse by a strong dose of parental frustration, anger, or worry.

Fortunately, we can use the following three steps to help our kids out of this unhealthy pattern:

STEP #1:
Take care of yourself when the conflict begins to erupt.
Instead of yelling, reasoning, or pleading, GRIN and say something like:

"Feel free to continue this argument some place where it doesn't hassle my eyes or ears. Outside or the basement. You

decide. Just try to keep the blood off of the carpet."

or

"Great fighting guys! But it hassles my eyes and ears. Are you going to take that someplace else? Or are you going to pay me to hear and see it? You decide."

or

"Uh oh! Is this going to be an energy drain for me?"

Your goal here is fourfold:
1. Surprise and confuse your kids with the response you give.
2. Prove that they can't control your emotions and gain attention by fighting.
3. Place responsibility for solving the problem on their shoulders.
4. Take the fun out of bickering or wrestling in front of you.

STEP #2:
If your kids continue to hassle your eyes and ears with fighting, develop a plan to help them pay you back for the problem.
Developing this plan involves the following steps:

a. Delay the consequence by saying:

"Uh oh. You guys didn't take it someplace else. I'm going to think about how you can both pay me back for this hassle. Maybe you can come up with something before I have to. We'll talk later. Try not to worry."

b. When you and your kids are calm meet with both and say:

"Remember yesterday when you wouldn't stop fighting around me? Have you decided what you are going to do to pay me for seeing and hearing it?"

c. If they can't think of what to do, give them some possible options, any and all of which will make you happy.

"Some kids decide to clean up the yard. Others wash the bathrooms. Some vacuum the carpets. Which one would work best for you?"

d. Give them a day or two to get the job done.

"Is it reasonable for you to get these things done by tonight or tomorrow night? Either time is OK with me."

Note: Never say, "Do it now!" The benefit of giving your kids a deadline of a day or two is that it gives you some breathing room. During this period, you have plenty of time to plan what you will do if your kids refuse or forget to do what you've asked! For more information on how to get chores done, see Chapter 3 "None of my friends have to do chores."

e. If the deadline expires, deliver sadness and a reasonable, logical consequence.

If one child has done something to pay you back, and the other has not, give a consequence only to the one who has not done something to repay you. BE CAREFUL TO AVOID COMPARING THE COMPLIANT CHILD WITH THE NONCOMPLIANT ONE!

Below are some examples of consequences:

"This is so sad. I guess I'll have to take one of your toys down to the pawn shop so I can pay someone to do the job."

"I'd love to take you to Silly Willie's Fun Park, but you didn't get your jobs done. I know it's hard."

"Your father and I are going on a date. I really need a break from your fighting. Mrs. Grumblesmythe from down the street will be watching you. She charges three dollars an hour if you are sweet or six dollars an hour if you're not. When she gets here, she'll ask you how you guys plan to pay her."

Note: When delivering these types of consequences, it is very easy to become sarcastic. AVOID SARCASM AT ALL COSTS!

Recently, we received a letter from a mom. In her letter she described how she and her husband used these very ideas to get a handle on their two sons' almost constant bickering, whining, and fighting. Her letter read something like this:

Dear Jim and Charles,

I'm writing this letter to tell you about my two sons. Mike is 8 years old, and Eric is 10. They used to argue and fight constantly, and my husband and I were about to pull our hair out. Then one night we decided to change our ways and use some of your Love and Logic instead.

This night, near the end of December, our boys wanted to go camping in the front yard. They wanted to set up their tent and pretend. Since it's been in the 20s and 30s at night lately, I told them that they could set up their tent in the living room or the basement instead. Boy did this ever start a fight! Eric wanted to camp in the basement, but Mike wanted to camp in the living room.

My husband and I decided to do what you told us. We stayed out of it and let them work it out. They did! At least we thought they did. Mike gave in to Eric, and they both ran off to the basement to arrange their campsite. My husband and I went to sleep. About 2:00 in the morning we heard a horrible sound. Eric and Mike ran into our bedroom pushing and shoving. Eric screamed, "Mom! Daaaad! Mike bit me!" Then he held up his arm. No blood but some pretty good marks.

Mike started screaming too, "He started it! He started it!"

My husband and I were so frustrated that we felt like strangling them. Instead, I remembered to use sadness instead of anger. I also remembered that it is OK to delay a consequence until you have a plan. I looked at the boys and said, "Oh no guys. Bad decision waking us up. Guess your father and I will have to do something about this tomorrow."

It was great! I'd never seen them look so confused. Then my husband said, "Go ahead and fight somewhere where it won't keep us awake."

When the boys continued to argue, I said, "The longer you keep us awake, the sadder it's going to be for you tomorrow."

The next morning, both of them came to us and asked us what we were going to do. My husband told them that they could take the day to think about how they might make it up to us by doing some chores.

When they got off the school bus in the afternoon, they came up the steps, ran into the house and told me that they'd figured out what they would do to pay us back for our loss of sleep. As they started to tell me, I stopped them and told them to wait so they could tell their father and myself together during dinner. I remembered what you told us about extending the consequence so that kids have to spend more time thinking about their problem. That's why I decided to let them stew about it until their dad got home.

During dinner, I could tell that both of them were about to explode. Finally they couldn't take it any longer and told us that they wanted to wash our cars to make up for the problem. We said, "That's a start. Throw in cleaning the bathtubs and toilets and we have a deal." The boys looked so relieved. They almost seemed thankful for the consequence!

Now when the boys start fighting, we just look at them and say something like, "This is so sad, I wonder if you'll need to do some chores to pay us back for all of this noise and hassle?" It's amazing how quickly they stop arguing. But, this doesn't always work. Sometimes they keep fighting. But that's good! When it doesn't work I get a break from some of my chores—the boys do them! Sometimes, when I'm really sick of housework, I even find myself looking forward to their fights!

Sincerely,

A happier mom

Another common cause of chronic sibling spats is when one child in the family feels compared to another, and he or she begins to feel like the "black sheep" of the family. When a child develops this perception, he or she reasons on an unconscious level, "I'll never be as good as my brother. Everybody thinks he's so smart—he's such a goody two shoes—I hate him!" In most cases the child doesn't really hate his or her sibling. Instead, they hate the feeling of not measuring up in the eyes of their parents or other important people. "Feeling" is the key word here, in that these perceptions or feelings are not necessarily accurate. The parents and other adults may not view the child in this manner. Nevertheless, the most important point is that the child "feels" it is so.

Growing up, I (Charles) had all sorts of difficulty learning in school. In contrast, my two older sisters were excellent students all the way through college. My parents never compared us. Unfortunately, my teachers did. "Your sisters were such good students" or "Are you as smart as your sister?" were common well-intentioned comments made at school. How do you suppose this affected my relationship with my sisters and my teachers? Sparing the ugly details, I wasn't a sweet little brother and I wasn't the teacher's pet.

Parents and teachers can do two things to help avoid this problem:

1. **Don't compare kids with each other.**

   One of the most damaging statements I ever heard was made in the local KMart store by a frustrated father, "Why can't you just sit and be good like your brother?"

2. **Celebrate your children's differences and focus primary energy on helping them identify and build upon their strengths.**

   Research clearly shows that personality and learning differences begin at or before birth. Therefore, just when you begin to understand how to parent your first child, a second one comes along who responds completely different. The more we try to make our kids the same, the more frustrated and angry everyone in the family becomes. Help all of your children learn that everyone is different, and that everyone has something positive to contribute.

   Lots of short conversations like the following can go a long way toward helping children feel good about themselves and their siblings:

Parent:	Do you think you and your sister are mostly the same or different?
Child:	I don't know.
Parent:	The other day you seemed pretty frustrated with the fact that she got some higher grades than you did.
Child:	I guess. I'm not a teacher's pet like she is.
Parent:	What are you really good at?
Child:	I don't know.
Parent:	You really like to draw?
Child:	Yeah?
Parent:	What are your favorite things to draw?
Child:	I like wild horses best.
Parent:	You might decide to be an artist some day. You are good at some things, and your sister is good at other things.
Child:	I guess.

Parent:	That's one of the things I love the most about you two. You're different.
Child:	But she gets better grades.
Parent:	(With a smile and a hug) Do you think that makes me love her more?
Child:	Naw.
Parent:	(With a smile and a big hug) That's right! I'll love both of you always!

Some thoughts on more severe forms of sibling conflict.
A final note on this subject has to do with much more serious and dangerous types of problems. In most cases, siblings call names, argue, whine, and occasionally hit each other. And, in most cases nobody suffers any irreparable harm. In rarer instances, one or more children in the family—or the entire family—is having such severe emotional distress that the rivalry has turned into dangerous, violent behavior. What's a parent to do if they see this happening with their children? Here are some suggestions:

1. **Supervise your children very closely, and do not ignore the problem.**

   Make sure that the children are adequately supervised and that they are not allowed to inflict serious damage upon each other. This is the one instance in which parents must intervene to ensure safety. Caution! With older children and teens, avoid trying to physically separate them. Call 911 or the police department for assistance if the conflict becomes violent.

2. **Remove any guns, knives, or potential weapons from the home.**

   Search your child's room to ensure that he or she does not possess anything dangerous. You have the right and responsibility to know what is in your child's room!

WISE WORDS
Wise parents keep their kids safe by knowing what is in their rooms. They merely explain to their children, "I'm your parent. It's my job to know."

3. Don't hesitate to get professional help!

There are solutions to these types of more serious sibling conflicts, but they require family therapy and ongoing work with a qualified mental health professional.

FOR YOUR THOUGHTS

1. In the history of humankind, has the statement, "Now say you're sorry and make up" every really worked?
2. Who has a big chunk of unhealthy control when a parent makes the mistake of asking, "Who started it?" The parent or the kids?
3. Why do kids fight when we are busy doing things like talking on the phone, cooking, spending time with our spouse, etc.? Could it be that at these times they feel lacking for our attention? Is there any more effective way of getting your parents' attention than instigating an exciting sibling spat?
4. How surprised will your kids be when you interrupt their next bout of bickering with, "Oh no! I just had an energy drain"?
5. When was the last time you spent some individual "alone time" with each of your kids? When was the last time you noticed each of their unique strengths—and shared these with them? See pages 172 for an example conversation.

CHAPTER 20

WISE WORDS

*Wise stepparents respond to this barb with,
"You're right! I'm not your real mom. But I do respect
you too much to argue. I'll do something about this
after I've talked with your dad (or mom)."*

What's a stepparent to say or do when he or she hears angry comments such as, "You can't make me! You're not my real mom!" or "I'm gonna go live with my real dad! At least he's cool"?

The power of these angry jabs lies in their ability to target stepparents' most common fears. Like verbal "smart bombs" these comments penetrate our deepest concerns and often create a stew of conflicting thoughts and feelings:

"How dare he say that to me!" (Anger)
"Uh oh! What have I got myself into here?" (Worry)
"Why won't she just do what I ask?" (Frustration)
"Why does he keep rejecting me this way?" (Hurt)
"I guess I should be more understanding." (Guilt)

The danger of these feelings comes from their ability to suck stepparents into one of two very common step parenting traps:

TRAP #1:
Being the "Buddy"
Out of guilt, sadness for the child, a need to be liked by the child, or a sincere desire to help, some stepparents fall into the trap of trying to be their stepchild's best friend. A voice inside of their heads seems to reason, "If I'm really nice, back off, and give him mostly what he wants, then he'll like me and we'll all get along." While their heart is in the right place, this strategy rarely brings a joyful ending. More commonly, sad things start happening to everyone in the family.

The first downfall of the "Buddy" approach is that it turns the biological parent into the bad guy or disciplinary "heavy." The parent is forced to do all of the discipline and to take the brunt of the child's frustration and anger. Soon he or she begins to feel resentment toward the stepparent and frustration toward the child.

The second pitfall of this approach is the effect it has on the child or children. The child feels anger and frustration toward the biological parent for being the heavy disciplinarian. The child also loses respect for the stepparent for failing to set limits. Yes! Despite their frequent complaints about limits, children DO NOT respect adults who fail to set them.

Finally, the stepparent experiences a sense of rejection from both the child and the biological parent. Despite all of their valiant attempts to keep peace with the child and to be friendly, both the child and the spouse are now very angry. The voice inside of the stepparent's head now speaks some very different words, "After all I've done for this family, nobody appreciates me."

TRAP #2:
Being the Bulldozer
Some stepparents find it very tempting to do the very opposite of the "Buddy" approach. Out of worry that the child will not respect them, to help an exhausted biological parent, falling back on how they themselves were parented, or as a result of sheer frustration, these stepparents fall into the trap of trying to bulldoze their way into the parenting role. In other words they resort to using anger, lectures, warnings, and threats with the child. Strangely, this "Bulldozer" strategy tends to create problems very similar to the "Buddy" approach—family relationships suffer.

First, serious power struggles develop between the stepparent and the child. In reaction, the biological parent often feels an urge to "cushion" or compensate for the stepparent's authoritarian rein by becoming more permissive or "buddy-like" to the child. Lastly, the marital relationship suffers as each adult feels unsupported by the other.

As we see below, the end result of both the "Buddy" and "Bulldozer" approaches is that they eventually push the family in separate directions.

Are you ready for some good news about stepparenting? Below are some tried and true tips:

Tips for Saving Stepparent Sanity:
1. DO NOT try to replace the child's "real" parent.
2. Focus only on what you can control—your own actions.
3. Give frequent injections of healthy control.
4. Neutralize the game of "divide and conquer".
5. Understand the loss stepchildren experience.

DO NOT try to replace the child's "real" parent.
The "Buddy" and "Bulldozer" approaches are ways that well-meaning people fall into the trap of trying to replace their stepchildren's "real" parent. Stepparents stumbling into these treacherous waters exert tremendous amounts of energy trying to control the uncontrollable—whether their stepkids accept, like, or respect them! As frustrating as it is, WE CANNOT CONTROL THE THOUGHTS AND FEELINGS OF ANOTHER PERSON! The more we try, the more frustrated everyone involved becomes.

WISE WORDS

The world's most powerful people focus the vast majority of their energy on what they can control beyond a shadow of a doubt—their own thoughts, feelings, and actions.

During one of my courses, a father stood up and commented, "I get it! I get it! I can't make my kids behave, but if I try real hard I can make myself behave!"

Laced with sarcasm, his wife grumbled, "That'll be the day."

Joking aside, this father's conclusion rings with truth. Telling kids to behave is fruitless. We truly cannot make another person behave! In contrast, showing others healthy behavior, describing what we will do and allow, and backing these limits with our own actions, brings many rewards.

The first step in setting limits in this way requires that we take a close and honest look at what we can and cannot control in our homes. Below are two lists. One of these contains controllable items. The other contains uncontrollable ones. Which one is which?

List #1
1. The tone of a child's voice
2. Whether a child takes out the trash
3. Who a child chooses for friends
4. Whether a child dyes his or her hair green

List #2
1. The tone of your voice—and whether you listen or don't listen to disrespectful talk
2. Whether or not you make deductions from the child's allowance for failing to do chores
3. Whether or not you set a healthy example by the types of friends you choose
4. Whether or not you pay for your child's hair dye

Wise stepparents focus most of their effort on list number two. They do this by following one simple rule:

NEVER TELL A KID WHAT TO DO.
TELL THEM WHAT YOU WILL DO INSTEAD.

Following this rule gets us into the habit of setting limits with enforceable statements "Enforceable Statements" are just what their name implies—statements describing limits we can actually enforce! Below are examples of stepparents using enforceable statements. Notice that the enforceable statements are highlighted in bold and italics.

EXAMPLE #1:
"You're not my real mom!"

Child:	You're not my real mom. You can't boss me around.
Stepparent:	(In a soft tone of voice) It's sad that you feel like I'm bossing you.
Child:	My real mom doesn't make me do this crap.
Stepparent:	***I'll be happy to listen to you when your voice sounds calm like mine.***
Child:	You're just using that psychology crap on me!
Stepparent:	(Still in a soft tone and beginning to walk away from the child) ***I'll be happy to listen when your voice is calm.***

EXAMPLE #2:
"But Dad lets me."

Child:	(In a calm tone) You said you would listen when I was calm.
Stepparent:	You bet. What did you want to tell me?
Child:	I don't see why you won't take me to R-rated movies. My dad does.
Stepparent:	Your dad takes you? That must be great fun.
Child:	Will you take me to that movie, "Death, Destruction, Sex and Mayhem"?
Stepparent:	*I'll be happy to take you to G-rated movies*
Child:	(Getting snippy) Well, I'll just go anyway!
Stepparent:	*I give allowance to kids who follow house rules.*
Child:	I don't care!
Stepparent:	(In a soft tone while walking away) Let me know what you decide.

Notice again that the enforceable statements focus on our own actions, whereas the unenforceable ones focus on the child's. Again, successful stepparents devote the most to what they can control—their own actions.

An added benefit of enforceable statements is the nearly magical way they help parents avoid power struggles with their kids. Most stepkids hate to be told what to do by their stepparent. It's as if a booming voice inside of their head says, "Who does this person think he is? He can't control me! No way!"

Control is an essential human emotional need. All people have a strong need for choice and freewill. Stepchildren often have even greater control needs as a result of the large number of things taking place in their lives over which they have no control. As more and more uncontrollable situations and changes take place around them, they become hungrier and hungrier for control. Below are listed just a few of the things over which stepchildren have no control:

1. Whether or not their parents got along and stayed married
2. Where they live and what school they have to go to

3. Who their biological parents choose as new partners
4. The financial changes that typically take place during and after the divorce
5. Whether they are able to see their old friends
6. How well (or not well) Mom and Dad cope with all of the changes and loss
7. What the new siblings will be like

When children become starved for control, they tend to react very poorly when people try to tell them what to do. It's almost as if three things start happening:

1. In their subconscious mind, a warning sounds, "CONTROL LOSS! CONTROL LOSS! CONTROL LOSS!"
2. They begin to ask themselves, "How can I get this control back?"
3. A menu of the following options pops up in their brain:
   a. "Should I act like I didn't hear what he said?"
   b. "Should I 'forget' to do it?"
   c. "Should I get belligerent and refuse to do it?"
   d. "Or, should I just do the opposite of what he told me to do?"

Regardless of the option chosen, both you and the child lose. The good news is that enforceable statements leave kids with a strong sense of control while at the same time allowing us to set firm limits.

Give frequent injections of healthy control.
Another strategy for avoiding power struggles involves giving your stepkids plenty of opportunities to make choices. Every time we allow a child to make a choice, we give them a little "injection" of control. Like medicine, sufficient doses go a long way toward healing parent-child relationship problems. As we mentioned, stepkids usually need a lot of these injections to compensate for all of the uncontrollable things that have happened in their lives

Unfortunately, many people seem to give their kids injections of unhealthy control. That is, they give their children choices on issues that create problems for others. Not too long ago, some friends of mine (Jim) came to dinner with their six-year-old son:

Child: (Throwing a fit at the table) I don't want to eat this! I don't like it!

Parent: Sweetie. Do you want to stay in your seat or come and sit on my lap?

Child: I want to sit in your lap.

Sixty seconds later

Child: I hate this food. Yuck.

Parent: I let you sit in my lap. Stop it.

Child: But I don't want to have this. I don't like it. When are we going home?

Parent: Do you want to sit in Dad's lap instead?

Child: I want Daddy.

Thirty seconds later

Child: I want Mommy.

Parent: Now calm down.

Child: But I want to go!

Where did these parents go wrong? Simply put, the choices they gave their son were the wrong types of choices to give a misbehaving child. Why? Because these choices created a major problem for everyone in the room. We had to listen to a crying and whining instead of each others' pleasant conversation! Clearly, the control they gave their son was NOT of the healthy sort. Listed below are some Love and Logic guidelines for giving healthy choices. Which ones did these parents violate?

Love and Logic Guidelines for Giving Choices
1. Give most of the choices when your kids are behaving well—not when they aren't.
2. Never give choices about dangerous issues.

3. Give two options with each choice. Each option should be OK with you.

4. If the child doesn't decide in ten seconds flat, decide for him or her.

5. When your child is misbehaving, or you really need to have your way, don't be afraid not to give a choice.

Here's an example of how a parent might use choices in a much healthier way:

Child: I don't want this stuff. I want to go home.
Stepparent: Can you act nice or would you rather spend some time in the other room?
Child: I want to go!
Stepparent: How sad. I guess you've chosen to leave us for a while. Come back and join us when you can be nice.

If the child is much older and is too large to be carried to another room...
Child: I want to go!
Stepparent: Can you be patient? Or will I need to do something about this when we get home?
Child: What are you gonna do? I want to go!
Stepparent: (In a calm, sad tone of voice) Your mom and I will talk and come up with something fair. Try not to worry about it right now."
Child: This is stupid!
Stepparent: The longer you argue, the sadder this is going to be.

Stepparents become even more powerful when they remember to give lots of small choices BEFORE their kids even begin to act up. Parent after parent has commented to us that doing this prevents most problems from even starting in the first place! But wait a minute! If the choices we give are mostly SMALL ones over SMALL issues, how can they have a BIG impact on our stepkid's willingness to cooperate? Simply put, small doses of control add up. Many small choices, given repeatedly over time, create a reservoir of control available to both the child and the parent. When a child experiences a healthy amount of control, he or she is much more likely to share some with the adult.

Examples of small choices include:
1. Would you like milk or juice for dinner?
2. Do you want to wear your coat or carry it?
3. Do you want to take out the trash tonight or in the morning?
4. Are you going to set your alarm for 6:00 or 6:15?
5. Would you like to be home by 8:30 or 9:30?

WISE WORDS
Control is a lot like love and respect.
The more we give, the more we receive.

Neutralize the Game of "Divide and Conquer"
Have you ever heard your kids say things like, "My mom lets me..." or "Dad told me that..." or "When I'm with my mom, she..."?

Have your ever said "No" to something your child wanted, just to find out that he or she asked your spouse just a bit later for the very same thing? And, has your spouse ever said "Yes," without knowing that you had already said "No"?

Has one of your children ever told your spouse that you gave them permission to do something that you really didn't? And, has your spouse ever blasted you for this before realizing the child had slightly "modified" the truth?

These situations aren't unique to stepparenting, and they don't mean that your kids are destined to become menaces. Anyone who's spent much time around kids has surely witnessed them experiment with the game of "Divide and Conquer." This game is relatively simple. There are three basic approaches. First, see if you can get what you want by comparing adults with each other and making them feel angry, confused, or guilty. Second, go from one adult to the next until one of them finally says, "Yes" to what you want. Thirdly, claim that one adult has given you permission to do something when they really haven't.

Most kids do not get up in the morning and plot, "I think I'll manipulate the adults around me so I can have my way." Instead, children who start to play these games fall into them by accident. All kids are scientists. All children look around at the world around them and wonder on an unconscious level, "I wonder what will happen if I do this? I wonder what will happen if I do that? How are these people going to react if I try this?" Through this type of experimentation, children either learn healthy or unhealthy strategies for relating to others and living their lives. When children find that manipulation works, they tend to make it a habit. When adults show them that manipulation doesn't work, they're forced to fall back on nicer ways of acting.

Stepchildren are particularly vulnerable to falling into the habit of using Divide and Conquer. One of their first unconscious experiments in the new family will be to test the fortitude of the marital relationship. In other words, they will do a number of rather frustrating things just to see how well you and your spouse can stick together as a team. Clearly, children desperately want their parents to be strong and support each other. When they see that it's relatively simple to get their parents bickering at each other, they begin to lose respect for each parent.

WISE WORDS
The more kids are able to control adults through manipulation, the more out of control they feel—and are!

How does a stepparent prevent their stepkids from falling into the habit of Divide and Conquer? Here are some tips:

1. Agree to argue about parenting only when the kids can't hear it or see it.
2. Avoid the "Buddy" and "Bulldozer" traps.

3. Treat manipulation as an "energy drain".
4. Whenever possible, consult your spouse before committing to something.

Agree to argue about parenting only when the kids can't hear or see it.
Parents often ask me, "What should I do if I disagree with something my spouse has said or done with the kids?" Our consistent answer?

WISE WORDS
Unless your spouse has done something downright abusive or neglectful, it is always best to support them in the eyes of the child.

Find a time when the child is asleep or out of the house to tell your spouse how you feel. Almost everyone disagrees at least a bit about raising children. And every parent makes mistakes. Occasional mistakes and typical disagreements don't damage kids. Seeing their parents argue about these mistakes and disagreements does!

Avoid the "Buddy" and "Bulldozer" traps.
The Buddy and Bulldozer stepparenting styles create fertile ground for manipulation through Divide and Conquer. In both cases, one parent becomes much stricter than the other. When this happens, children sense this marital friction and fall into the trap of pitting parent and stepparent against each other.

Treat manipulation as an energy drain.
A friend of ours has a stepson who was the master of deception. When he turned ten, he had a birthday party, invited almost all of the kids in his class, and made quite a killing on gifts. In fact, it took two cars to get all the packages home from the park where the party was held. Surveying his cache, his mother and stepfather agreed that he ought to donate a small number of the

items to a local children's charity. The boy agreed, and picked-out a few toys that were still in the manufacturer's packaging. What a sweet child! Well, almost.

The next morning the boy got up before Mom and Stepdad, went to the garage where these toys were stored, and opened every one. When his mother woke from her slumber, he showed her the opened toys and said, "Look what Dad said I could open." The excitement was just beginning! What happened? Mom confronted Stepdad, who was quite surprised and perplexed by her anger. Dad snapped back. Soon both of them realized they'd been "had" by a ten-year-old. What a bummer!

Whenever possible, consult your spouse before committing to something.

When your stepkids come asking for something, experiment with saying the following BEFORE making a decision:

"I can't give you an answer yet. Your mom and I will have to talk first."

or

"I'll let you know just as soon as I've talked to your dad."

WARNING! Your stepkids probably won't thank you for this! Children want answers fast, and they might just get pretty mad having to wait around as you and Mom ponder the merits of their requests. Nevertheless, when you do this, it accomplishes many noble things. First, you stay out of hot water with your spouse. Second, your kids will soon realize that their parents will always back each other up. Third, you model a very healthy approach to problem-solving—taking time to consult with others before making a decision.

Understand the Numerous Losses Stepchildren Experience.
When humans lose anything significant, they grieve. We experience grief from losses of many types, including the loss of treasured possessions, pets, familiar places, comforting routines, friends, and loved ones. The amount of grief we feel

depends on both the magnitude of the loss and how many other losses we've recently had. Stepchildren often experience high levels of grief due to the multiple losses they experience.

From research studying the effects of loss, we know that people go through a number of difficult emotional stages as they grieve. Stepparents can help their kids AND save their own sanity by being aware of these stages and having some practical techniques for dealing with problems as they arise. Most importantly, we must be kind and empathetic while at the same time never excusing misbehavior.

WISE WORDS
Wise parents empathize with feelings but don't excuse misbehavior.

Stages of Loss for Stepkids:

STAGE #1: Denial
During this stage, the child may deny that they are upset about any of the losses or changes that have taken place in their life. In fact, they may actually believe that they don't care. This stage might also be termed the honeymoon stage. What is my advice to stepparents? Enjoy it, but don't be surprised if it doesn't last.

STAGE #2: Anger
This is not a fun stage for anyone! Gradually, the honeymoon fades away, and the hard reality begins to set in. It is not unusual at this stage for kids to become very irritable, mouthy, and even defiant. Their anger is expressed in the form of arguments, such as:

I hate you. Don't try to be my parent!
I wish you never married my dad!
Why are you always on my case, my real dad is cool!
You can't tell me what to do. You're not my real mom!

Luckily, this stage is temporary, IF adults respond in a firm yet loving way. But, what's a stepparent to say when they hear things like this? Here's an example:

Child: I wish you never married my dad!
Stepparent: You wish that your parents were still together?
Child: Yes! I hate you.
Stepparent: (In a sincere, sad tone) I'm sorry you feel that way.
Child: But I do.
Stepparent: I'm sorry you feel that way. I can understand that this whole thing has been really tough for you. I'll be happy to listen when I feel like we aren't arguing.

STAGE #3: Bargaining

During the bargaining stage, people experiencing loss try to make the uncomfortable situation go away. At this stage, step kids tend to say things like:

I'm gonna go live with Dad!
I'm living with my friends. This family sucks!

What's a parent to say?
Child: I'm out of here!
Stepparent: Where are you going?
Child: I'm gonna go live with Dad!"
Stepparent: (With warmth and sincerely) I will love you regardless of where you decide to live.

STAGE #4: Sadness

When the child realizes that the loss will not go away, he or she often goes through a period of sadness or depression. At this stage it is essential that both parents merely listen and provide support. The more loved the child feels, and the more we listen to and accept their feelings, the faster they will move on to happier times. See Chapter 4 "Our Kids are Hurting and Need to Talk About Difficult Things" for some ideas about how to listen when kids are hurting.

STAGE #5: Acceptance

This is the reward to everyone in your family for all the hard work they have done! At this stage, the child begins to see you and the entire situation as livable. Keep up the hard work. It's worth it!

FOR YOUR THOUGHTS

1. How do many kids respond when their stepparents try to tell them what to do?
2. Why is this? Can we really control what kids do and how they behave? What are the only things we can actually control?
3. What are some of the negative things that happen when stepparents try too hard to make their stepchildren happy? What happens when stepparents take the opposite approach and become Bulldozers?
4. How do stepchildren test the strength of the new marital relationship? Does "Divide and Conquer" ring a bell?
5. In example #2 on page 180, the parent did not try to argue about whether it was proper for the child's father to take him to R-rated movies. Stepmom even commented, "That must be great fun." Why is it so important to avoid debating with a child whether the actions of another adult are proper or improper? Might this be a losing battle?

CHAPTER 21

WISE WORDS

Wise parents recognize "guilt trips" from their kids, and they never give in to this type of manipulation.

"You hate me!" is often one of the most surprising and upsetting "hooks" that our kids cast our way. The power of these three simple words comes from their ability to shock us and to unconsciously trick us into doing more thinking than the child. As we grapple with a multitude of conflicting thoughts and feelings, our kids sit back and relax.

As their kids pry into their hearts with "You hate me!" many parents describe the following series of conflicting thoughts and feelings:

"How can he say that after all I've done for him?" (Hurt)

"Where does he get off saying this?" (Anger)

"Maybe I've done something to make him feel this way." (Concern)

"I haven't been spending enough time with him." (Guilt)

"I've been too hard on him." (Guilt)

"But he's just trying to manipulate me!" (Anger)

"But if I were more sensitive..." (Guilt)

These thoughts and feelings are like quicksand. The more we struggle with them, the more exhausted we get and the deeper we sink. Sadly, our children also get stuck when this happens—stuck into using guilt to get what they want.

This trap is easy to slip into because of some very common parenting myths.

A COMMON "YOU HATE ME!" MYTH.
I should always have positive feelings for my child.

While cleaning-up after one child, talking to the school principal about another's poor behavior, and responding to something like, "I'm the only kid who has to do chores," how many parents sometimes fantasize about a much simpler life? Parenting is by far the most challenging and unrelenting type of activity known to humankind. Nevertheless, many good and loving parents feel extremely guilty when they occasionally experience negative feelings toward their children—and when they temporarily wish it would "all just go away."

When parents beat-up on themselves with guilt over these unspoken feelings, their kids are quick to recognize it. Isn't it amazing how well children can read their parent's body language? Each time they hear a tinge of guilt in the tone of our voice, and each time they see it on our face, they file it away for future reference. "You hate me!" represents one way that kids unconsciously use this guilt to gain unhealthy control over their parents. That is, the power of "You hate me!" comes from its ability to trigger fears and guilt related to situations in which the parent REALLY HAS felt anger, resentment, or even hatred about something the child has done.

The sad paradox is that this parental guilt frequently results in a vicious cycle, in which the parent actually becomes less and less loving toward the child. That is, the more guilt a parent feels, the more likely that the child will gain unhealthy control over that parent. And, the more the child controls the parent, the more likely the parent will experience even greater feelings of anger, resentment, or frustration. The parent's greatest fears soon become reality, with the child becoming less and less fun to be around. Don't fall into this trap!

WISE WORDS
Wise parents know that the better they take care of themselves, the more love they will have for their children.

Give yourself a break! No matter how much we love and cherish each of our kids, sometimes they do things that we really do hate! Accepting these feelings as normal is the first step. The second step involves putting ourselves first in a loving way by setting firm limits and by allowing our children to own and solve their own problems. Parents who do this—and resist the urge to argue with "You hate me," see some magical things happen. They begin to feel less anger, less frustration, and less guilt. They also begin to see happier and more responsible kids!

ANOTHER COMMON PARENTING MYTH
My child should always like and love me.

Emerging from the economic prosperity of the late nineteen fifties and the "if it feels good, do it" philosophy of the nineteen sixties, came a pervasive societal belief that parents were placed on earth to make sure that their kids are always happy and always have what they want. As a result of this societal conditioning, many parents are now very afraid of "damaging" their children by upsetting them. As a result, they really do damage them by "stealing" any opportunities for the child to learn about real world struggles and consequences. Please don't steal from your child!

WISE WORDS
Wise parents know that NOT getting one's way from time to time is actually good practice for life! Children who are always protected from being upset become always upset adults.

Down deep in their souls, kids are really most happy when they have to earn what they want and are not allowed to run the house. Nevertheless, if a child is anywhere close to being normal, he or she will occasionally experiment with "You hate me" to see if the parent crumbles with guilt. If the parent stands firm in a loving way, the child learns a very healthy lesson about life: "You don't always get what you want—and that's just the way it is. Nothing personal." In contrast, if the parent gives in, the child learns something very unhealthy: "When you don't get what you want, it's unfair and mean. But if you cry, whine or argue, people might just give-in."

A THIRD PARENTING MYTH
What my child says when angry must be true.

A basic psychological rule of thumb states that people don't make much sense after they've guzzled a twelve-pack of beer. Would you put much stock in what a person says when they're drunk? Of course not! When people are drunk, what they say is generally nonsense. The same principle applies to children who are "drunk" on frustration, anger, or rage. Under these conditions, "You hate me" really means "I'm so mad at you that I'll say almost anything to hurt you or get my way— regardless of whether I really mean it!"

Although it makes NO sense to reason or argue with an angry child, in the heat of the moment it's easy to slip into this hole. How do parents avoid this trap? Many find it easier to resist verbal warfare or guilt when they remember the following:

WISE WORDS
Never reason with a drunk.

Reasoning with someone's emotions is like fighting fire with lighter fluid. It just doesn't work! Instead of calming the person, reasoning or arguing makes the person even hotter. Instead of feeding the flames, successful parents do four things when their kids make angry comments:

Four basic skills for responding to an angry child
1. Listen and really try to understand how the child is really feeling.
2. Name the child's feelings, using simple statements such as, "It sounds like you're really mad" or "It seems like you are really angry about this."
3. Continue to listen with empathy, use Love and Logic One Liners, and repeat skill #2 as needed.
4. If the child continues to argue, walk away while saying calmly, "I love you too much to argue. I'll be happy to listen when you are calm."

Below is an example of a how a Love and Logic parent might respond to a fairly calm child who tries "You don't love me!"

Child: You don't love me!
Parent: (In a sincere, caring tone) You're really upset.

Child:	You never loved me.
Parent:	(Still calm and sincere) I'm sorry you feel that way.
Child:	If you loved me, you wouldn't be so hard on me.
Parent:	I'm sorry you feel that way.
Child:	Stop saying that!
Parent:	I'll listen when your voice is calm like mine.
Child:	Whatever! (Storms off to his room)

Here's another example with a much angrier and older teenager:

Teen:	You hate me!
Parent:	You're really mad about the car.
Teen:	This sucks! If you really loved me you wouldn't make me pay for the damage.
Parent:	You hate this.
Teen:	You know I hate this! Besides, Jason's parents bought him a new car when he wrecked his.
Parent:	You wish I'd do that?
Teen:	Yeah! If you cared about me, you'd buy me another car instead of making me pay for fixing that ugly piece of crap!
Parent:	(Walking away) I love you too much to fight with you about this. I'll be happy to listen to you when both of us are calm.
Teen:	I want to talk about it NOW!
Parent:	(Without saying a word, continues to walk away)

Parent after parent has commented to us how well this type of approach works. They find that their kids are always much easier to deal with after they have had some time to calm down. Then some healthy problem solving can take place!

WISE WORDS
Angry people need three things: Empathy, space, and time to cool down. The only person who can really calm an angry person is that person.

FOR YOUR THOUGHTS

1. What happens when parents fall into the trap of believing that they should always have positive feelings toward their children?
2. When is it most tempting to talk with your child about a problem?
   a. When he or she is still angry and won't really hear a word you say?
   b. After he or she has calmed down and will listen?
3. When is the BEST time to talk with your child about a problem?
   a. When he or she is still angry and won't really hear a word you say?
   b. After he or she has calmed down and will listen?
4. What is a child really saying when they yell, "You hate me"? For a clue to the answer, see page 195.
5. Who is the only person who can really calm an angry person?

CHAPTER 22

WISE WORDS

In boredom are the seeds of creativity. Wise parents allow their kids to get bored, and they help them channel this feeling into creative discoveries.

How many times does the average parent hear, "This is booooring!" or "I'm boooored." before their kids grow up and leave home? And have you ever known a kid (or adult for that matter) that seemed to exist in a vacuum of perpetual boredom? Have times ever changed! Years past, kids really knew better than letting anyone know they were bored. They knew beyond a shadow of doubt that uttering the words, "I'm bored" or "This is boring" was an open invitation for some adult to say, "Oh goodie!" and hand them a rake, shovel, dust cloth, broom, or some other instrument of childhood despair.

A major shift in thinking has taken place in America. It wasn't long ago when the vast majority of people believed that it was their own personal responsibility to find happiness in life. Nobody else was expected to make it happen for them. They understood that contentment is an inside job. When a person was bored, they had to find something to keep themselves busy. It was just that simple.

Today many hold a vastly different mindset. Their logic seems to follow the opposite course. "People should entertain me. It's not fair if things are dull. Somebody needs to make sure that I don't get bored. If I'm unhappy it's somebody else's fault." Sadly, people holding these beliefs spend most of their time feeling frustrated.

Where have these new beliefs come from? Reading the newspaper, I (Charles) came upon an advertisement describing a summer program for kids. It read something like this, "Only you (meaning parents) can prevent a boring summer!" The ad went on to describe the wonderful things your child should be doing instead of sitting around being bored with you. More and more, parents are being sent the message that it is bad if their kids get bored. Advertisements, the yuppie parents across the street, and misquoted research sends the same message, "You are a bad parent if you don't keep your kids emerged day-to-day, hour-to-hour in a highly entertaining environment." Hogwash! Where would we be today if someone had made sure that Ben Franklin or Thomas Edison never got bored?

WISE WORDS

The more we entertain kids, the more they will start to believe they need to be entertained.

It is clear from good, solid research that kids' brains do develop better when they are exposed to a wide array of stimulating experiences. Unfortunately, our society seems to have confused healthy stimulation with entertainment. Healthy stimulation includes a variety of activities that encourage kids to think. Some of these activities include reading your children books, telling them stories about your childhood and their ancestors, asking them questions about their day, playing games with them, etc. And, "stimulation" doesn't always require adult participation. Some of the most valuable activities involve children playing alone with materials or toys that foster creativity. These very healthy materials and toys share two characteristics. First, they don't have batteries. Secondly, they can be played with and used in a variety of interesting and creative ways. Here are some examples:

Examples of Materials and Toys That Foster Creativity
1. A sandbox
2. Clay
3. Dolls and toy animals (without batteries)
4. Books
5. Crayons, paints, markers, and paper
6. Toy cars and trucks that you have to push
7. Wood and safe hand tools for woodworking (for older kids)
8. An old cardboard box (Believe it or not!)

Using the materials and toys listed above requires active thought and creativity. Entertainment, in contrast, is passive in nature. In small doses entertainment is healthy and important! How many of us occasionally go to the movies or watch a TV show just to "get away" from the daily grind or something that's worrying us? Unfortunately, too many children are bombarded with entertaining toys and activities on a daily basis. What effect is this having? Across the country, teachers continually report that more and more kids are hyperactive, expect to be entertained, and have difficulty with self-directed thought and creativity. In my (Charles') own work as a therapist, I've seen

many children who've never really learned to play creatively!
One five-year-old walked into my office full of the toys and
materials suggested above, picked up a rag doll, pushed on it,
and began to shake it around. In disgust, he threw it on the
floor, plopped down in a chair, and complained, "Booooring!
Batteries dead." Listed below are examples of toys and
activities that should be limited by parents. In small doses,
they are healthy and fun. When they become a way of life,
they are harmful.

Examples of Toys and Activities which Discourage Creativity— and Encourage Boredom

1. Video games
2. Television (Even watching educational shows or videos does not require ACTIVE thought, creativity, and participation.)
3. Toys that talk too much and have too many flashing lights
4. Too many daily schedules which look something like:

Morning:	Get dressed, eat breakfast, go to soccer practice
Midday:	Grab fast food lunch on the way from soccer practice to the swimming pool
Afternoon:	On the way to Karate class, go by the store to pick up brownie mix for tomorrow's Boy Scouts meeting
Evening:	Get home from Karate and get ready for dinner with neighbor family
Night:	Have dinner, go home, pass out

If this schedule looks familiar, give yourself and your kids
a break!

WISE WORDS

*More is not always better. Exciting, entertaining
activities are great fun, but wise parents also know
that quiet times are just as important!*

Most adults will admit that parts of their jobs are pretty dull.

Life can be fairly boring at times, particularly when we're trying to complete a rather long task or reach an important long-term goal. Because many children have been exposed to a constant barrage of stimulating activities, they are unable or unwilling to tolerate this delayed gratification, or "boredom." They have no patience for it. These are the kids that find it extremely difficult or even painful to complete book reports and other more lengthy school assignments. They find the boredom of initial planning stages difficult, and they often lack the creative problem-solving skills necessary to jump hurdles as the task unfolds. What can parents do to avoid this trap? Listed below are some suggestions.

Tips for encouraging creativity, problem-solving skills, and patience in your home
1. Limit television viewing, watching videos, and playing video games.
2. Fill your home with materials and toys that foster creativity.
3. Purposefully develop "Boredom Training Sessions."

WISE WORDS
The ability to tolerate boredom and to entertain oneself are essential life skills. Like any other abilities, practice makes perfect.

Limit television viewing, watching videos, and playing video games.
Nothing can compete with the constant audio and visual stimulation provided by the latest video games, fast-paced television shows, and special effects clogged movies! Even the most energetic and well-trained teachers on the planet find it practically impossible to compete with the sheer entertainment value and momentum of these electronic wonders. What price are we paying here? What type of an impact must excess exposure to these activities be having on children's attention spans, their ability or willingness to tolerate boredom, and

their overall ability to succeed in less consistently entertaining settings such as school or the workplace?

There are no sensible reasons for children to spend more than thirty minutes to one hour each day engaged in these activities. Even the viewing of educational television shows does not require ACTIVE participation, frustration tolerance, or creativity.

Wait a minute! Aren't watching TV and playing video games both civil liberties protected for children by the U. S. Constitution? Not really, but some kids like to argue they are! Let's take a look at how a friend of ours weaned her kids off of these activities—and dealt with their attempts to argue her into backing down:

Child:	I'm bored. Can I watch TV?
Parent:	I'm worried about leakage.
Child:	What? What are you talking about?
Parent:	I'm not sure you want to hear about it. It's pretty scary.
Child:	What?
Parent:	Are you sure you want to hear?
Child:	Yes. Tell me!
Parent:	Well, OK. When kids watch too much TV or play too many video games, something really horrible happens. (Parent stops here and holds out a long pause)
Child:	(Getting just a bit frustrated by the parents' pauses) What?
Parent:	Leakage. Yeah leakage. Their brains get so soft and mushy that they start to drain out of the ears. It's horrible, and it makes a big mess all around the house.
Child:	(Rolling her eyes) Mom! That's dumb. Can I watch TV?
Parent:	(Shaking head "No" and smiling) What kind of a parent would I be if I cared so little that your brains leaked out? How could I live with myself?

Child: But I want to watch Mutant Death Squad. Please?
Parent: (Still smiling) Maybe some other time. What kind
            of a parent would I be?
Child: Not fair!
Parent: (In a calm yet firm tone) What kind of parent
            would I be?
Child: But this is sooo dumb!
Parent: (Giving the child a hug) I love you too much to see
            your brains leak. And, I love you too much to argue.
            Maybe we should just get rid of that dangerous TV
            set if it causes these types of arguments.
Child: (Walks away very quietly)

**Make your home rich with materials and toys that
foster creativity.**
Listed on page 201 are some examples of materials and toys that
foster creativity. Three nice things about them is that they are
typically less expensive, tend to make a lot less noise and don't
require batteries! Even more importantly, they give children
essential opportunities to create their own entertainment and
learn by doing—rather than merely watching. Research has
clearly documented that this type of active learning is essential
for healthy brain development and visual-motor coordination.

Purposefully develop "Boredom Training Sessions."
What in the world is a "Boredom Training Session" or BTS?
Exactly what it sounds like! Simply put, children need practice
learning how to entertain themselves in creative ways. Kids
who never get this practice tend to become easily bored,
unhappy, and rather difficult to be around when things get
"boring." A BTS is a planned opportunity for children to
find themselves in a dull situation, get bored, and create their
own excitement.

When the types of materials recommended above are made
available, many kids quickly enter their own world of creativity
and imaginative thought. It is through this process of being in
a dull situation, becoming uncomfortable, and creating one's

own enjoyment that children develop many of the self-control and problem-solving skills necessary for success in school, interpersonal relationships, and work.

Some kids seem to adapt pretty easily to these sessions. They go off by themselves and play without much of a struggle. Unfortunately, other children don't make it quite so easy for their parents! How children react to a Boredom Training Session depends on a number of factors. These include their inborn temperament or personality characteristics, how "addicted" they've become to highly entertaining electronic devices and toys, and how much experience they've had with creating their own entertainment through creative play. For any child, the key to success is planning. Listed below are some tips.

Basics of Planning a Boredom Training Session or BTS:
1. Pick a time that is convenient for you.
2. Consider how your child might react.
3. Put three key Love and Logic tools in your back pocket.
4. Provide a dull period of time in your home.
5. Watch your child learn and grow!

Pick a time that is convenient for you.
Obviously, some days and times are better than others for a Boredom Training Session. Which of the options below sounds best to you?
   a. When you're exhausted with a terrible head cold?
   b. The evening in April while you're trying to finish your tax return?
   c. When you are paying bills and the checkbook won't balance?
   d. When you're well-rested, relaxed, and have time to supervise the session?

All but the most "adventurous" parents typically choose option "d"!

Consider how your child might react.
"I WANT TO WATCH TV! THIS IS BORING! JOE'S MOM
LETS HIM DO FUN STUFF. WHY ARE YOU SO MEAN!
WHAT AM I SUPPOSED TO DO? I CAN'T THINK OF
ANYTHING TO DO."

WISE WORDS
*Wise parents never try something new with
their kids before they've asked themselves,
"How might my child react?" and "What might go
wrong with my plan?" Successful parents find the holes
and plug them—before they launch the boat!*

Many kids seem to be masters at the art of finding loopholes
in their parents' plans and short-circuiting them with arguing
and manipulation. The same goes for a BTS. Easily bored
children will typically start an argument, repeatedly whine,
or misbehave in some other way. As soon as the parent gets
sucked in to the fray, the child is no longer bored! What
could be more exciting than an entertaining display of parental
frustration or anger?

Most parents are really good at predicting how their children are going to react to a BTS. The key to surviving—and
helping your child—is having a plan just in case your child
starts his or her own unique brand of water torture. Discussed
below are three BTS parent survival skills.

BTS Survival Skill #1:
Handing the "boredom problem" back in a loving way
What do average, red-blooded American kids do when they
first fall within the dreaded grips of boredom? Most start
dragging. They drag on over to one toy. They drag on over to
another. They drag outside. They drag inside. Finally, they drag
over to one of their parents, frown, and complain, "I'm bored.
There's nothing to do. Can I watch TV?" When the caring
parent responds with a simple, "No," the whine intensifies and

becomes something like, "But this is booooooring. There's nothing to doooooooo."

I've never met an honest parent who didn't have some fantasies about what they'd like to say to their kids in response. Listed below are some ideas. Which one fits with Love and Logic?

    a. "I'm sick and tired of this whining. When I was a kid, we had to make our own toys out of worn-out shoes."

    b. "Go tell your mother."

    c. "Well....OK. You can watch TV...but just this one time...and stay off the cable channels!"

    d. "It's hard to be bored. What are you going to do?"

Obviously, idea "d" fits best with Love and Logic! The first essential tool for a successful BTS involves handing the problem back in a loving way.

WISE WORDS

Wise parents hand the "boredom problem" right back to their kids in a loving way. In response to, "This is boooring!" smart parents ask with empathy, "What are you going to do?"

Every time we expect a child to solve his or her own problems, and provide loving guidance as they struggle, we give a priceless gift! Each time we resist the urge to jump in and fix problems for our kids, they walk away with a little more wisdom and self-confidence. Every time they encounter a problem, struggle, and succeed, they can look back and reason, "I did it! I've got what it takes!"

All of this sounds nice and fine, but how does a real-life parent actually pull this off? It's time for another example.

Child: This is boooooooring! I'm bored.

Parent: (In a sincere tone) That sure sounds like a bummer. What are you going to do?

Child: (Shrugging her shoulders) I don't know.
           Watch videos?
Parent: What a bummer. No videos for now. Would you
           like some other ideas?
Child: What?
Parent: When some kids get bored, they ask their parents if
           they can do chores. How would that work for you?
Child: Horrible! I don't want to do chores.
Parent: Some kids decide to go play in the sand and make
           pretend games. How would that work?
Child: (Silent)
Parent: Other kids go make things with clay, crayons,
           paper, or something else. How would that work?
Child: That stuff is all boring stuff.
Parent: What a bummer. I bet a smart kid like you will
           figure something out. Let me know how it goes.
           (The parent gives the child a hug and walks away)

Note: What's really interesting is that many kids will respond this way yet end up doing one of the things their parent had suggested. Smart parents don't try to make the child decide right away. Instead, they give some options and keep putting the problem back on the child's shoulders.

This parent's approach is summed up in the five steps below. While reading, keep in mind that this tool works with all types of problems—not just boredom. Any time a child has a problem, or creates one, wise parents fall back on the following five steps.

Step #1: Show that you care and understand.
     That sure sounds like a bummer.
Step #2: Hand the problem back in a loving way.
     What are you going to do?
Step #3: Find out if the child wants some suggestions.
     Would you like some other ideas?
Step #4: If so, give two or three potential solutions.
     When some kids get bored, they try _____. How would that work?

Step #5: Allow the child to solve the problem.
I bet a smart kid like you will figure something out.
Let me know how it goes.

These five steps are extremely powerful, but what's a parent to say or do if their child insists on arguing and whining? Some kids try to short-circuit this tool by constantly saying things like, "That won't work" or "That's a dumb idea" or "I just want to watch TV!"

CAUTION #1: DO NOT fall into the trap of giving more and more suggestions as your child sits back and mumbles, "Won't work. Won't work. Won't work."

CAUTION #2: DO NOT fall into the trap of lecturing or arguing if your child begins to argue, whine, or refuses to solve the problem. If you are arguing or lecturing, the entire goal of the BTS is defeated—your child is no longer bored! For a bored child, a nice argument, some parental lectures or threats, or even an angry look can be just the entertainment they want. Therefore, the single most important part of planning a BTS is making certain that the child is unable to spice things up for themselves by getting their parents pulled into a battle.

BTS Survival Skill #2:
Ending arguing and manipulation by going "Brain Dead"
Fruits, vegetables, rocks, and twigs all have one thing in common. They don't think! Love and Logic parents share this characteristic as soon as their kids start manipulating—they go "brain dead". Kids can't argue with a grape, and kids can't argue with a brain dead parent. Brain dead parents are also VERY booooring! Why? Simply because they just calmly repeat the same thing over and over again—instead of arguing or getting mad. A close friend of ours started doing BTS's with his ten-year-old daughter. Let's take a look at how he went "brain dead" when the youngster started arguing.

Child: I'm bored.

Parent:	That stinks. I hate being bored too. What are you going to do?
Child:	Let's go to Silly Pete's Pizza!
Parent:	I'd love to, but not today. We are eating here at home.
Child:	Mom's right. You ARE selfish! When I'm with her, SHE takes me places.
Parent:	(In a soft, calm tone of voice) I love you too much to argue.
Child:	But I'm starving to death! You never do anything fun with me.
Parent:	(In an even softer and more boring tone) I love you too much to argue.
Child:	But not fair!
Parent:	(In a sad tone) This is so unfortunate. Is this going to be an energy drain? Or are you going to stop arguing?
Child:	(Runs quietly into her room)

How did Dad keep his cool? First, he lost all brain function and kept repeating the Love and Logic One Liner, "I love you too much to argue" Secondly, when the manipulation continued, he simply asked, "Is this going to be an energy drain for me? Or are you going to stop whining and arguing?"

BTS Survival Skill #3:
The "Energy Drain" technique

What's a parent to say or do if the first two tools don't work, and their child continues to argue or misbehave? One of the quickest ways to deal with any continued manipulation, arguing, or misbehavior is by requiring some type of payment for the inconvenience or "energy drain" resulting from them. The goal is to make the payment fit the crime. In other words, what the child is expected to do should seem logical and reasonable. Listed below are some ideas for repayment. While reading these, keep in mind the importance of delivering such consequences with empathy.

1. Do some of their parents' chores like cleaning toilets, vacuuming, etc.
2. Use their own money or possessions to hire someone else to do these chores.
3. Use their own money, do extra chores, or give up possessions to hire their own babysitter. Meanwhile, the parents go out and have fun.
4. Parent rests at home, instead of taking the child someplace fun like the movies, the amusement park, etc.

Obviously, the daughter in the previous example above had some previous experience with putting energy back into her father. She opted to stop being nasty immediately after her father asked, "Is this going to be an energy drain?" Throughout this book, we have given many examples of this approach. For another example of this technique in action, see Chapter 6: "#$%$@#@*%" (Swearing).

Begin the BTS by providing a dull period of time in your home
Are you ready to have some fun? After you've chosen a convenient time, considered how your child might react, and put the three most essential BTS tools in your back pocket, it's time to get started! Peace and quite is the rule here. That's it! A "dull period of time" just means between thirty minutes to an hour of simple peace and quiet once every day. During this time there should be no highly entertaining activities, such as watching television, playing video games, surfing the Web, riding in the car from one activity to the next, eating fast food, running around the house with a friend, or blasting the stereo.

Wait! Isn't this child abuse? Might a kid's brain just explode from the lack of electronic exposure? Is it truly possible that a child might actually get "bored to death?" All joking aside, these sessions can be pretty tough for children who are not accustomed to finding creative ways of entertaining themselves. Therefore, parents are often wise to start with very brief sessions and gradually increase their length over a period of one or two weeks.

Notice and Enjoy the Behaviors You Want

There is nothing more exciting than watching one's child engrossed in their own play or some other creative activity! Sneak up on them sometime and watch for a while. If you really like what you see, show them that you've noticed it. What does this mean? When your child is doing a good job entertaining him or herself, walk over and briefly describe what you notice them doing. Here are some examples:

I noticed you can make animals out of that clay!
I noticed you are playing all by yourself!
I noticed you like to draw with those colors!
I noticed you are pretending that this box is a spaceship!
I noticed you're reading about dinosaurs!
I noticed you are resting!
I noticed you put Teddy in jail!

WARNING! DO NOT end each statement with something like, "...and that's great." The power of this technique comes from the child feeling noticed—NOT judged. Even a positive judgment such as, "That's nice," implies that you are more interested in the product or outcome of the activity than who is performing it. When kids feel "noticed" for these simple activities, their self-esteem soars, and they begin to enjoy and take pride in entertaining themselves. What we also tend to see is a calmer and more content child—and we don't end up spending so much on batteries!

FOR YOUR THOUGHTS

1. What is the difference between healthy stimulation and entertainment?
2. Did you notice how the parent on pages 204-205 used humor by talking about the brain "leakage" caused by excess TV viewing? When parents use fun humor like this, does it show their kids that parents can be in control of the

home in a loving, calm and confident way?

3. What might happen if a parent tried to have a Boredom Training Session without doing some careful planning first? Is it possible that their child might find a hole in the plan? Could the entire thing blow up in a very bad way?

4. Is a child bored if they can see their parent angry and frustrated? Is a child bored if they can get their parent to argue?

5. Why is it so important to "notice" when your kids are doing a good job of entertaining themselves?

CHAPTER 23

Thanks for caring enough about your kids to read this book! Parents like you are making the world a better place for generations to come. Unfortunately, we have all known other parents who aren't really giving their children what they need—love, limits, and logical consequences. Often, they find great sounding ways of explaining away their responsibility to provide these essential ingredients in the lives of their kids. One of the most famous excuses goes like this, "I know kids are going to drink. I'd rather know where they are and that they are safe. So I rented a hotel room for their after-prom party. At least I'll know that they won't be out on the streets getting into trouble."

This parent is not only taking the easy road, but is violating the law so that he won't have to take a stand on what is right and wrong. This parent is asking for trouble. He might as well be there serving the drinks and encouraging inappropriate behavior. Not only is he giving permission for underage drinking, he is actually encouraging his kid's law-breaking by financing the escapade.

It takes a strong parent to stand firm for what's right. And, it's getting harder and harder each year as more parents in our neighborhoods fail to provide limits for their kids. Almost every youngster can point out other parents who allow their kids to drive without licenses, drink, stay out all night, go on unsupervised coed trips, party without adult chaperones, etc.

Today's youth have developed many great sounding, but intellectually immature, arguments. These seem to be designed to go right to the heart of loving parents and weaken the resolve of the best of us.

Typical Manipulative Arguments

You just don't want me to grow up.

All the other parents understand.

Don't you trust me?

All the other kids get to do it. Their parents aren't so overprotective.

It's only a little party. You should appreciate that I'm not like those bad kids that always get wasted out of their heads with drugs.

WISE WORDS
Wise parents know that arguments such as these are not requests to hear parental wisdom. Instead, they are designed to weaken parent's resolve and get one's way.

One of the major goals of this book has been to remind parents that we do not try to match wits with kids when they get into the arguing mode. When kids lock into manipulative arguments, they are not listening to see if we have something wise to add to the conversation. They are listening only to hear us give in. Anything short of this only makes them more determined and more manipulative.

In the event that the adult does not give in, the usual teen response is anger and/or demonstrations of hurt.

I hate you!

The only reason I don't have any friends is because of you!

I'm waiting for the first teenager in history to respond with, "Your argument makes a lot of sense. Thanks for sharing your wisdom with me. I know it takes a lot of love on your part to set limits when it's right. I know that I'll be a better person for staying away from that party. Give me a hug."

When this happens, we will know that it's time to retire. Until then, we'll keep writing books and giving lectures. Something tells us we'll be at it for quite some time!

WISE WORDS
It is easier and more effective to tell kids WHEN they CAN do something—instead of than telling them "No" or lecturing.

My (Jim's) mother had this technique refined to an art form. I can remember that one of my greatest desires was to ride my bicycle in the street just like all the other kids. She could have lectured me about the fact that this kind of activity was extremely dangerous for someone my age. In fact she did just that. She carefully explained why it was not safe. She even mentioned that the drivers might not be as careful as I thought I was. This did not work. I didn't listen. I had all the answers. I was invincible.

Mom was a quick study. She soon learned from experience that I wasn't going to listen. Even the most thoughtful, brilliant lecture would not have worked. My heart was set on riding in the street! Besides, she knew just what I'd say, "It won't happen to me. I'm careful. I'm not like those reckless kids who ride out in front of our house. I'm not a baby anymore. When are you going to let me grow up? You just don't want me to have any fun. Just because you never had a bike, you don't know what it's like."

Mom had neither the time nor the energy to listen to my arguments, so she took another approach. Let's take a look.

Little Jimmy:	Mom. The other kids ride their bikes in the street. Why can't I?
Mom:	I want you to ride in the street. And as soon as you are 13 years old you can do it.
Little Jimmy:	(Thinking I could wear her down) But that's not fair!
Mom:	(Very calmly) OK—13 years, 6 months old
Little Jimmy:	(Not prepared for Mom's tactic) But—but.
Mom:	(Still very calm) Do you want to go for 14 years old? I think I'd like that a lot better. In fact I have no desire to see you in the street with that bike until you've had some driving experience. I'm willing to go with 13 years old as long as I hear no more about it. Each time you bring it up or argue, I'm adding 6 months."

Needless to say, the case was closed and the day I turned 13 was a great day. I was enjoying the freedom of riding in the street. Down deep, I was also very thankful that my mother, Marie, loved me enough to set limits.

The "You Can" Technique
My (Jim's) mom had stumbled onto a great technique, and being a quick study, she used it often. I remember statements such as:

Jimmy, you can make up the house rules when you have your own home.

Jimmy, you can smoke after you graduate from high school.

Jimmy, you can drink when you're married. (I think she even added, You'll need it then.)

Jimmy, you can have a car when you can buy it yourself.

Jimmy, you can use those words when you're not in the house.

Jimmy, you can stay out as late as you want when you are 18.

Jimmy, you can go to all night parties as long as you invite your mom and dad.

WISE WORDS
The best technique in the world won't work if your kids believe that you won't back your words with actions.

This technique was effective for my mother because she had laid the foundation for good parenting when I was young. She never made idle threats. Her word was gold.

Shortly after I gained the privilege of riding in the street, my newfound freedom was too much for me to handle. I was feeling quite independent. As the proud owner of both a bicycle and a Denver Post paper route, I had my own money and could spend extended amounts of time away from home.

One Saturday I took off for a ride to the park, met my girlfriend's family and stayed for a very long time. Suddenly, I realized that I had forgotten to let my mom know where I was and when I'd be back.

The glow of this freedom was tarnished immediately upon my return home. Mom was furious, and without warning, locked up my bike for 30 days. All the money I made that month delivering papers was spent renting a bike from a friend so I could keep my paper route. If I didn't believe my mom was running the house before this, I sure knew it now!

Did this experience cause me to hate my mother? Did it cause me to become self-destructive to get even with her? Absolutely not! I was mad. I told all my friends how mean she was. Then—I got over it and gained a lot more respect for her at the same time.

As I look back on the experience, I can see how much easier it would have been for her to not take a strong stand on responsibility. But that would have been the same as stealing one of life's great lessons from her son. I now know that it took a lot of love on her part to do what she did.

A Great Gift

As I reflect on this experience, I realize now why I didn't make a habit out of forgetting to tell my mom where I was going. I also realize that her totally unpredicted action of locking up my bike left me forever with a sneaking suspicion that there was no limit to what she might do. I did know one thing for sure—that she'd always back her words with actions. I didn't thank her for it at the time, but what a great gift she gave me. I didn't have to waste a lot of my time arguing and misbehaving in order for her to set and enforce limits. Instead, we maintained a life-long relationship of love and respect.

Applying the "You Can" Technique

Let's take another look at the all night party request and see how a parent might apply the "You Can" technique. Before we do, however, it's smart to consider the following:

WISE WORDS
Wise parents know that doing the right thing won't guarantee a happy kid.

Teen: Mom. Dad. Guess what? Randy's dad got us a room at the hotel so that we can have a great after-prom party. It's going to be so awesome. All the kids are going to be there. Please say I can go. Please!

Parents: Can we assume that Randy's dad is going to be there?

Teen: Of course not. This is an after-prom party. He's just getting us the room. It's not like when you went to school. Kids are a lot more grown-up now.

Parents: We thought you knew how we feel about unsupervised parties.

Teen: But this is different. All kids do this after the prom.

Parents: You can attend all the unsupervised parties you want as soon as you're living on your own.

Teen: But that's not fair. All the other kids get to do it.

Note: At this point, it's time for parents to fall back on the "I'm (we're) sure that's true. And..." approach.

Parents: We're sure that's true. And when can you attend the all night parties?

Teen: When I'm on my own. But we're just going to be talking!

Parents: We're sure that's true. And when do you get to attend all night parties?

Teen; You're so old-fashioned.

Parents: We're sure that's true. And when do you get to do that?

Teen: What am I supposed to do, tell my friends that my parents treat me like a baby?

Parents: You might consider asking them to provide adult supervision, and then you could join them for the party. You can go to those kinds of parties either when you are living on your own or when there is adult supervision.

WISE WORDS
Wise parents remember their civic responsibility to report unlawful activities.

Have horrible tragedies resulted from activities taking place during unsupervised teen parties? Have kids, left to drive home under the influence of alcohol or drugs, killed others and themselves? Have the lives of many families been devastated because of these accidents?

We've talked to parents who knew that underage drinking was happening and did not report it to the authorities. These parents admit that the reason they did not intervene was that they were afraid that their children would be mad if they got involved.

These same parents now realize that the length of time their teen would have been mad was nothing compared to the long-term guilt and pain they'd feel knowing that they could have prevented a tragic accident.

Help your kids learn early in life about your civic responsibility to report any dangerous or criminal activity. Say to your kids, "Tell your friends not to take it personally if we report underage drinking. It's our civic responsibility. It simply has to do with saving lives. That's all."

FOR YOUR THOUGHTS

1. Consider how much you agree with the following statement. "Kids need parents who can be their friends."
2. Is the following statement more accurate than the last? "Kids need parents who provide firm limits, do the 'right thing' even when it's the 'hard thing,' and show plenty of warmth and love in the process."
3. Considering the two statements above, which parent raises kids with the strongest character?
4. Which of the following statements will create the least resistance?
   Statement A:
   "You are not going to use the car until you've paid for your share of the insurance."
   Statement B:
   "You can use the car when you've paid for your share of the insurance."

5. Will kids thank us for using the "You Can" approach? Probably not, but will we feel proud of ourselves for holding firm in a loving way?

......♥......

Index

One-upmanship game, avoiding, xiii
Over-controlling parents, problems
  for, 78, 86-87

Painful memories, 49, 114-15
Parental influence, U of, 76, 77
Parental kudos, fixes of, 136
Parent-child relationships, 181;
  building, 18, 76, 131, 193-94,
  220; damaging, 10, 53, 56-57, 78
Parenting, arguing about, 185, 186
Parties: after-prom, 216, 220, 221;
  all-night, 117, 118, 119, 219;
  unsupervised, 221-22
Patience, developing, 203
Pearls, Fritz: on children as psychia-
  trists, 13-14
Peer pressure, 115; dealing with, 57,
  80-82; over-controlling parents
  and, 86-87; problems with, 75-76
Personal appearance, 23
Physical development, concerns
  about, 27
Plans, 141, 142; consequences and,
  109-10; making, 9-10, 39
Police, calling, 153, 155
Positive feelings; beliefs about, 197;
  maintaining, 192
Positive messages, sending, 80-81
Pouting, 2; abandoning, 116
Power struggles, 91; avoiding, 10-11;
  creating, 97; food issue, 28; neutralizing, xxvii, 124; stepparents
  and, 177. See also Struggles
Pride, 45
Problems: fixing, 20, 23-26, 41-42;
  ownership of, xxiv, 24
Problem solving, 62-63; healthy
  approach to, 187; learning, xx,
  xxi-xxii, 49, 203, 210; responsi-

bility for, 167; among siblings,
  165; skills for, 206; thinking out
  loud and, 55
Professional help. See Mental health
  professionals
Public melt downs, 143; energy
  drains and, 42
Punishment, 69; avoiding, 150; drug
  use and, 151, 152

Quiet times, entertainment and,
  202-3

Real world, learning about, 162,
  194
Reasoning, anger and, 195, 197;
  avoiding, 161, 195
Recharging, chores and, 110, 111
Reinforcers, 93
Rejection: pain of, 28, 44, 114, 115;
  triggering feelings of, 158
Relationships: building, xvi-xvii,
  xviii, 145; denial and, 150; main-
  taining, ix, 17
Remaining calm, 17, 56, 73-74,
  109-10, 116, 140, 154, 155, 195;
  importance of, 179
Reminders. See Warnings
Rescuing, consequences of, xxi
Resentment, 193; building, xxiv, 45,
  56, 65; consequences and, 128
Respect, x; arguing and, 175;
  destroying, 4; gaining, 46, 220
Responses: Love and Logic, x, xiii;
  suggested, ix-x; surprising/confus-
  ing with, 167
Responsibility, xxiv, 81, 215; civic,
  117, 119, 221-22; development
  of, xxii, 46, 54, 74, 95, 159;
  drug use and, 152; excuses and,

· ·

Love and Logic Seminars

Jim and Charles Fay, Ph.D. present
Love and Logic® seminars and personal appearances
for both parents and educators in
many cities each year.

For more information,
contact Love and Logic® at:

1-800-338-4065

or visit our Web site:

www.loveandlogic.com